HERBALISM
for WITCHES

Create Your Magical Garden While Discovering The Hidden Power of Plants Through Spells, Rituals and Remedies for Your Body and Spirit

Avril le Roux

© Copyright 2022 by Avril le Roux - All rights reserved.

All rights reserved. No part of this book may be reproduced in any form without permission in writing from the author. Reviewers may quote brief passages in reviews.

While all attempts have been made to verify the information provided in this publication, neither the author nor the publisher assumes any responsibility for errors, omissions, or contrary interpretation of the subject matter herein.

The views expressed in this publication are those of the author alone and should not be taken as expert instruction or commands. The reader is responsible for his or her own actions, as well as his or her own interpretation of the material found within this publication.

Adherence to all applicable laws and regulations, including international, federal, state and local governing professional licensing, business practices, advertising, and all other aspects of doing business in the US, Canada or any other jurisdiction is the sole responsibility of the reader and consumer.

Neither the author nor the publisher assumes any responsibility or liability whatsoever on behalf of the consumer or reader of this material. Any perceived slight of any individual or organization is purely unintentional.

About Me

Welcome to the Other Side of the Veil

A world whispered of and often misunderstood. Avril le Roux invites you to explore the truths, dispel the myths, and see the full potential of modern witchcraft. Follow her journey as she brings to life years of practice starting with her very first breath.

Gifted by her mother, Avril discovered her creative power through magical traditions dating back centuries. The older she grew the more she began to experiment on her own, adding her unique nuances to this storied craft. Today, Avril strives to bring understanding to the role and uses of witchcraft, its powers and benefits, to the rest of the world.

Her books are the continuation of her personal education and research, and the slightest hint of mischief on a cool autumn day. Avril strives to bring a bias-free light to the magic surrounding us, ages-old spells, and rituals designed to help you chart a spiritual path.

Fierce, determined, funny, Avril hopes you find the magic spark within as you begin your journey to enlightenment and, if done right, awakening.

Table of Contents

Foreword 9
Introduction 10
Chapter 1. The Power of Nature 13
Chapter 2. Grow Your Magic Garden 21
    Pure Magic at Your Fingertips 22
    How to Setup Your Magic Garden 23
    The Power of Seasons 26
        Yule (December 21) 27
        Imbolc (February 2) 27
        Ostara (March 21) 28
        Beltane (May 1) 28
        Litha (June 21) 28
        Lughnasadh (August 1) 28
        Mabon (Semptember 21) 29
        Samhain (October 31) 29
    Final Thoughts 30
Chapter 3. Herbs & Magical Recipes 31
    Gathering & storing herbs 32
    The Witch's Herbarium 34
        A 34
        B 34
        C 34
        D 35
        E 35
        F 35
        G 35
        H 36
        I 36
        J 36

- K. 36
- L. 36
- M. 37
- N. 37
- O. 37
- P. 37
- R. 38
- S. 38
- T. 38
- V. 38
- W. 38
- Y. 38

Herbarium of poisonous herbs 39
- Aconitum 39
- Belladonna 39
- Hemlock 40
- Black hellebore 40
- Henbane 40
- Mandrake 41
- Stramonium 41

The 15 Essential Herbs for Witches 42
- Laurel 42
- Mugwort 43
- Basil 44
- Chamomille 45
- Cinnamon 46
- Jasmine 47
- Lavender 49
- Mint 50
- Rose 51
- Rosemary 52
- Sage 53

- *Dandelion* 54
- *Thyme* 55
- *Verbena* 56
- *Enchant your herbs* 57

Chapter 4. Magical Infusions 58
- *To Manifest Prosperity* 59
- *To Attract Money* 59
- *To Attract True Love* 60
- *To seduce someone* 60
- *To heal a broken heart* 61
- *To gain wisdom* 61
- *To bring mental clarity* 62
- *To strengthen your health* 62
- *To break the evil eye* 63
- *To get good luck* 63
- *To break jealousy* 64
- *To tackle laziness* 64
- *To break avarice* 65
- *To achieve inner calm* 65
- *To improve inner balance* 66
- *Final Thoughts* 67

Chapter 5. Become a Natural Healer 68
- *Consumption methods of natural magic remedies* 70
  - *Infusion* 70
  - *Decoctions* 70
  - *Oils (non-food use)* 70
  - *Tinctures* 70
  - *Pouches* 71
  - *Baths* 71
  - *Incenses* 71
- *Terapeutic Herbs* 72
  - *Essential Oils* 74

- *Distillation* 75
- *Maceration* 75

Herbal Healing Decoctions 77
- *Inluuence with fever* 77
- *Cold* 78
- *Nausea* 78
- *Digestion issues* 79
- *Cough and Influence* 79
- *Antioxidant and vitaminizing decoction* 80
- *Purifying decoction* 80
- *Draining decoction* 81
- *Soothing decoction for inflammations* 81
- *Energizing and stimulating decoction* 82

Magickal Pouches 83
- *To ward off negative energies* 83
- *To strengthen your love bond* 83
- *To raise financial well-being* 84
- *To foster spiritual enlightenment* 84
- *To propitiate prosperity* 85
- *To healing spiritual wounds* 85
- *To deepen gratitude* 86
- *To instill self-confidence* 86
- *To develop a magnetic appeal* 87
- *To develop self-control* 87
- *To induce sound sleep* 88
- *To foster passionate love* 89
- *To calm body and mind* 89
- *To attract honesty and sincerity* 90
- *To reverse mental and psychic fatigue* 91

Final Thoughts 92

CONCLUSION 93

FOREWORD

Since the dawn of time, human beings have mastered the magical art of herbalism, using magical herbs and plants in their daily lives: from purely culinary use to medical and mystical use, the sacred power of green magic has seen Mother Nature open to boundless horizons.

No cult, religion, or tradition in its history has not made use of herbal magic, adapting to its path the best method of using this outstanding and immeasurable ally. Even in ancient times, early humans began to understand the fascinating properties of herbs and plants, experimenting with their healing and magical properties. It was primarily women who were in charge of gathering and preparing herbs useful for physical survival - but also spiritual - employing healing herbs through the fumes of ancient incense that allowed them to communicate with the ancestral deities. Traditional witchcraft - but also Wicca - has kept intact the herbal traditions of distant eras, continuing to pass down from generation to generation the teachings of the ancestral witches; even today, the magical use of plants and herbs is pervasive in all witchcraft practices.

But green magic, if at first it was branded as heresy in the Dark Ages, became a natural science with the passing of centuries, revalued by monks and Christian priests, and finally accepted and spread as an all-natural medical discipline - modern herbalism. For as long as humanity can remember, magical herbs have always represented the sacred connection between body and spirit, material and the invisible, between man and their gods. Ancient civilizations such as the Egyptians, the Romans, the Greeks, and most of the peoples who have made history, burned fragrant incense on their altars in pursuit of communion with the deities. Through magical plants, each propitiated something different and necessary: from divination to find out the results of the harvest, to tribute to ingratiate themselves with the gods, to use to promote healing.

Today, magical herbs and spells are often connected, intertwined like the serpents of the caduceus so that every witch can benefit from all their immense esoteric potential. It is not strange to see how most rituals and magic spells often require blends of enchanted herbs to increase their effectiveness. Herbal magic accompanies witches and wizards of every Age, and each of us, today may be fortunate enough to practice what is - for all intents and purposes - a magical science.

INTRODUCTION

Welcome to the Witch's Herbarium, dear friends. Together we will embark upon a journey into the magic of herbs through easy explanations and powerful spells to start your practice on the right foot. Dive into the mysteries and ancient properties of flowers and plants while learning how to use them to create herbal potions and natural remedies and become a Green Witch.

I have dedicated my life to these special arts and hope you will share every step of your journey in my thrill. Start with an introduction to Green Magic, its history through the centuries, and the beliefs and religions that revered - and still revere -Nature. This dates back to the Celtic culture. Learn who the Druids were and how, in modern times, Nature worship evolved into the Wiccan religion. You will also be taught how to tune in to Nature, and the most common myths about who should and should not be a Witch will be debunked.

Continue on with unique insights and practical applications as you are guided through the creation of your magical garden. There are immense powers to be gained from cultivating your magical ingredients. You will also learn about the magic of the seasons and the Wheel of the Year, or the Witch's calendar, which differs from the traditional one we all know and rely on daily. You will discover the holidays that occur during the Wheel of the Year, called Sabbats, and gain the proper knowledge to honor these feast days through ancient pagan traditions. By now, your blood should be flowing a little faster. Perhaps an electric jolt in your heart as you envision the possibilities awaiting you. In chapter three, you will learn how to collect plants and herbs in a conscientious and environmentally friendly way and store them properly to be used in creating your spells. You will be provided with a herbarium with the main plants used in potion making and their magical properties to begin to become familiar with the magical power of the plants you already know and discover new ones. You will also be provided with a herbarium of toxic herbs to learn how to recognize and avoid them and discover how they were used in ancient times for therapeutic purposes and beyond. Then you will be provided with a veritable grimoire with authentic recipes for magical infusions and natural spells to propitiate love, prosperity, healing, luck, and more. My goal is that you can start right away to try your hand at creating magical recipes, even without prior experience.

In chapter four, you will find out who the natural healer is, what they do, and how you can become one. Being a natural healer is more than having a cursory knowledge of herbs and their properties. It is the ability to create powerful herbal remedies to heal people conscientiously, effectively, and professionally. You will receive a list of herbal remedies introducing you to natural healing and consuming methods.

Being a Green Witch is a calling linked to the Earth's roots. Often this affinity for mother-earth is felt at an early age. There are children who, more than others, love to be barefoot in the grass, feel peace in the middle of a forest (especially at night), adore water-from the sea to simple mud-filled puddles-spend afternoons climbing trees, and sometimes go so far as to talk to the entities that inhabit green areas. It is a frequent symptom of feeling connected from an early age with nature, seeking peace even in the shade of a tree in the middle of a metropolis. But becoming a Green Witch is not just about having a strong affinity with Nature; it is a conscious choice.

To choose to become a Green Witch is to vote one's life to Nature, in which to live peacefully and in harmony with it; it is the choice to honor Mother Earth every day, to feel grateful for every new flower that blooms, for every blade of grass that sprouts, for the water that flows copiously down river courses. Although anyone can learn the art of making magic through plants, becoming a natural healer requires a sensitivity and predisposition common to few. You have likely felt your inner calling by now: the need to explore this world and gain valuable insights for your magical practice but no doubt have questions and doubts. Let's answer some of the most prevalent ones together. Many are

⚹ **I cannot be a Nature Witch if I live in the city or away from nature.** False! Where you live has nothing to do with your abilities. You could live in the middle of nature and not be able to take care of a cactus, or live in an apartment in Manhattan and feel the need to have your living space filled with lush, healthy plants.

⚹ **Only women can be Witches.** Of course, they can't! A witch has male and female valences, but if "witch" in the masculine form doesn't appeal to you, you can call yourself a Witch! Witchcraft has no gender, race, age, or social status limitations.

⚹ **I didn't hear the "call" as a child.** I'm an adult now, is it too late? No, it is never too late. Not everyone feels the "call" from an early age. It also depends a lot on the environment you grew up in and the beliefs that were instilled in you. If you feel that this is a path you want to take now, it simply means that you are now ready to receive such knowledge. Witchcraft has no age. Ultimately, Witchcraft is not a path you can go down on a whim or for fashion, because it would lead nowhere. It is nature itself that calls you, when you are eligible to connect with it, regardless of everything else. What matters is answering that call, and if you are reading these lines, it means you have done that, and I love you for it. I wish you a good reading from the depths of my heart.

Welcome, my friends. I hope you will enjoy this journey as much as I have and that you will be enlightened about the greater natural world.

Avril le Roux

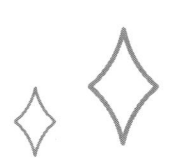

Chapter 1
The Power of Nature

Green Magic is the oldest of all forms of Witchcraft, with roots going back to early prehistoric religions. It is easy to see how Green Magic may have been the first used by man, as in ancient times, people lived in close contact with nature and used it to survive, heal from illnesses, and in several cases, connect with the deepest part of themselves. Moreover, a man respected it, sought ways to understand and control it to benefit from it, and at the same time, was incredibly fascinated by it. That is why in every religion of antiquity, we find the worship of nature: the elements, atmospheric phenomena such as rain and snow, the sun and the moon, were worshipped, but rituals were also held to avert natural disasters such as volcanic eruptions or earthquakes. Prehistoric man's life was based on nature, its rhythms, and cycles. Man had to adapt to it, learn to understand it and thrive through its knowledge.

When approaching the wonderful world of esotericism and witchcraft, it is very common to come across the discovery of the existence of different forms of magic. We refer, in particular, to the four colors of magic: white, red, black, and green. Each of these forms represents the magical intent contained in the will of each witch. Magic, you will realize, has no color: it is one, branching out through each initiate's use of it. Why then speak of "the colors of magic"? The answer is simple.

Real spells, rituals, and magical formulas can fall into different contexts; each witch can choose whether to direct her Will toward magics dedicated to well-being - her own and others' - or toward so-called "dark" magics. The colors of magic relate solely and exclusively to each practitioner's use of magic. It is a method, coined long ago for distinguishing the intentions with which one acts and emphasizing a certain aspect of it. White magic, red magic, black magic and green magic are subtle ramifications of one immense power: that of will. Green Magic, in its highest forms, is the most powerful practicable by man. It arises from and merges with the whole, overcoming dualistic concepts of Good and Evil and returning to the beginning of being. Therefore, it is only up to one's ethics to choose whether to employ the tools offered by Nature to raise one's creative potential and act for a higher purpose.

Historical Notes

Green Magic traces its roots to the Celtic religion. Unfortunately, there is very little historical evidence about the Celts. Since they were non-writing people, we have few direct records of who they were and what they did. Much of what we know about the Celts is due to the Romans and Greeks, whose historians have spoken extensively about their culture and customs. That of the Celts was a polytheistic religion, where both male and female deities were worshiped, and their worships were conducted in direct contact with Nature. The Celts considered forests sacred and revered water. There was no difference between the material and the spiritual: matter itself was a manifestation of the divine. Around 1700, writers and poets gradually began to take an interest in the Celtic people, including folkloric elements of Celtic culture in their stories.

Unfortunately, the Celts were forgotten over the centuries, as was their worship of Nature, as religions began to veer to the idea of a better world beyond earthly life, rather than focusing on the world around us. In recent years, however, there has been something of an awakening, perhaps partly due to the realization that man has largely mistreated nature and we now suffer the consequences. Many people have recently approached the natural world, realizing what a valuable help it can give us in life, for in nature lies life itself. Without Nature, there would be no life. Today, various cults and religions have incorporated these forms of Nature reverence, such as Wicca and Neo-Druidism. Let's take a look at these two faiths.

Wicca

Wicca is a belief directly descended from the Celts, i.e., it adopts their principles of Nature worship but simultaneously deviates greatly from the original aspects of Celtic culture. The Celts used to practice haruspicy, the divinatory art where animals were sacrificed and their entrails were read to interpret omens, just as human sacrifices in honor of the god Toutatis were not uncommon; Wiccans do none of this, do not sacrifice animals and do not practice violence in general. The only rule of Wicca is, "As long as you do not harm, you can do anything," and from this commandment comes the Law of Three, which can be summarized as: "Everything we do comes back to us three times for good and three times for evil." Therefore, if you act in good you will receive three times the good, if you act in evil you will receive three times the evil. This is why Wiccans do not practice Black Magic, expecting the evil inflicted to return three times as much. The founding father of Wicca is believed to be Gerald Gardner, a writer and essayist who devoted his life to spreading the Wiccan religion. Thanks to him, Wicca quickly spread throughout Europe and much of North America. Wicca's religion is based on opposing the two cosmic principles, the God and the Goddess, which together form the One. There is a strong belief in reincarnation in Wicca, which is generally characterized by deeply rooted ethics. Life and death are opposites but are seen in the form of a circle, so it is not just death that follows life, but life that follows death, and this is where the strong belief in reincarnation originates as a direct consequence of the cyclicality of existence. Since this is a religion in its own right, one must go through a real conversion to become a Wiccan. Before becoming a Wiccan, one must go through a long study, meditation and practice journey.

Neo-Druidism (or Modern Druidism)

Neo-Druidism is based on the Druidism practiced by Celtic priests. As with the Celts, we have no direct accounts of the druids, and what we know of them today is drawn from accounts of Greeks and Romans and accounts of Irish amanuensis monks. The reason for not leaving writings was the exclusivity: the druids passed on their knowledge orally and to a select few, affirm so that the secrecy of their traditions would be maintained. As mentioned in the chapter on Wicca, druids used to practice animal sacrifices to foretell the future and often human sacrifices as a good omen in battle.

Some sources testify that the druids gathered in Gaul every year to discuss important spiritual and political issues. Druids were not only priests but often also held positions of social and political importance, which is why the Romans later persecuted them. As also happened toward Christianity, the reason the Romans persecuted the Druids was political and not religious. Druidism began to disappear in Gaul and Britain because of the legions and the spread of Christianity. At the same time, it persisted in Ireland under the consent of Bishop Patricius, who the Pope commissioned to evangelize the population.

Shamanism

Shamanism is one of the oldest spiritual practices in the world, the father of cults that have spanned History, and the ancestor of contemporary spiritualities. For as long as we can remember, it has been a complex of traditions and beliefs aimed primarily at the theme of both physical and spiritual healing. Shamanism's primary purpose is to bring balance and harmony in body, spirit, and the visible and invisible worlds. It is precisely by keeping the natural world, that is, the visible and material world-in balance with the invisible and ethereal world that complete peace and harmony can be achieved. From its earliest days, this is what Shamanism teaches us: the pursuit of well-being through the sacred balance between the worlds.

The word shaman comes from the language of the Evenki, a small Tungus-speaking Siberian group. This word was originally used about a religious figure found in that region, but as early as North America, it was applied to a category of healers. A broader definition that could identify the shaman (or female shamaness) could expand to include all those people who exercise control over the trance state. The shaman is generally considered a healer who heals the soul and body through the help of both nature and the supernatural. The shaman is, in effect, a mediator between the two worlds, the bridge that allows the spirit to reach the earth and vice versa. It is precisely through the alteration of consciousness-known as the trance state-that the shaman can travel into the spiritual dimensions so that he can bring-when he returns-messages from the spirits, words of power, pearls of wisdom, and healing remedies. Today, Shamanism is a spiritual practice still alive all over the world. It has existed for as long as man has existed because it was born out of the collective consciousness of men and evolved with it as a function of the men who practice it. Shamanic practices and journeys allow us to explore the unconscious to discover ourselves to understand the deep mechanisms that animate us. Understanding our discomforts and removing blocks that cause anger, fears, and illnesses allows us to discover our weak points and restore balance. In this way, we can evolve and advance along our spiritual path.

Green Magic as a Path

When one begins to study something by going back to its history and traditions, it is easy to begin to wonder if there are rules and dogmas to be followed to take that particular path. For Green Magic, as well as Witchcraft in general, this is not the case. Wicca and Neo-Druidism are just two of dozens of cults and beliefs related to Nature and have been explained to you in this book for educational purposes only. This does not mean that to become a Green Witch or practice Witchcraft, you must convert to a particular religion. Whatever creed or religion you belong to (or even if you do not practice or believe in any religion), there is no reason you should have to change anything about who you are to practice Witchcraft. Beginner practitioners often confuse Witchcraft and Wicca by indiscriminately using these two terms. Still, one of the key differences is that Witchcraft is Wicca is a religion, a spiritual path, and a set of beliefs aimed at creating a harmonious and balanced way of life, while Witchcraft is a set of practices and rituals.

Witchcraft, which is the pivot of this book, is developed by keeping an open mind and far from adhering to religion in specific. This does not mean that, if you desire to do so, you cannot decide to be part of one creed rather than another. Witchcraft has no limits except that of your conscience. But don't worry if you still feel lost at the moment and have no idea what direction to take. It is more than normal, when starting on a path, to feel overwhelmed by the thousands of possibilities offered to us. The wisest thing to do is, in such cases, to take the time to study and investigate finally until you have sufficient knowledge to make a thoughtful and convincing choice that will change your existence forever.

Tuning in to Nature

One of the first steps for a Green Witch is to tune in to the nature around her. This is easier if forests and natural parks surround one, but it is not a fundamental aspect. With the right techniques and connection, a green witch has no difficulty tuning in to nature even if she is on the 20th floor of a skyscraper in the center of a metropolis. But how to tune in? One of the practices that is most useful for this purpose is meditation. It is necessary to be focused in the present moment, firmly grounded with mind and body to our surroundings. Being aware of our surroundings makes us more responsive to the energies that permeate them and the vibrations it produces, but not only that. Being present also means aligning one's vibration with the surrounding vibration to reconnect with the universe and merge into one.

When you feel nervous, angry, sad, or extremely euphoric, it will be very difficult to tune in to Nature's vibrations, which vibrate with stillness, balance, and harmony. Therefore, you must first balance yourself and your emotions and only then attempt to successfully connect to Nature. To do this, you can sit cross-legged on a comfortable superfice. Inhale deeply three times, exhaling slowly. Feel the energy pervade your body; do not judge it, just observe it. Focus on your breath, relax every part of your body starting with your head, neck, shoulders, abdomen, pelvis, legs, feet. Visualize a ball of golden light from the center of your abdomen and radiating along your body's extremities, healing you. Feel all negative emotions slipping away from your body as the golden light gives you a sense of peace, absolute stillness. Now that your body is vibrating at a high frequency visualize the golden light turning bright green. The green light colors every cell in your body, flows first to your feet, radiates outside your body, into the earth you are sitting on, and flows embracing everything it encounters. Green energy connects you with the ground, with nature. You are now tuned to it.

Not all Green Witches see or perceive the world in the same way-it is also what makes us unique. What matters is that you are connected with Nature and understand what it requires of you. You have to create a special connection with it. Living in a skyscraper or the open country makes little difference to your Green Witch abilities. Instead, you must accept the environment and become one with it. If you are in a noisy, crowded city, the only way you can connect with it is to accept it for what it is. It will do you no good to imagine different realities. Similarly, you must be able to accept the changes your environment constantly faces: a change of seasons, moon phases, new neighbors, an imported tree planted in the condo garden, a new park with an artificial pond across the street...

To connect with your environment, you need to use all five senses. When something new enters your environment touch it, smell it, observe it, taste it (if it is edible) and infine listen to the noise it makes. You must be open to knowledge. After giving proper attention on the fixed fixed plane, you can move on to the spiritual one. What vibrations does it send you? How does it make you feel? Connecting to the natural world gives you the ability to have access to the energy around you and use it for your benefit.

Final Thoughts

In this introductory chapter we learned about Herbalism through history, discovering that Nature Worship and Green Magic have very deep roots dating back to Celtic religion. We delved into Wicca and Druidism to give you a glimpse of the main features of these beliefs compared to Witchcraft's freedom of faith.

Finally we talked about what it means to attune to Nature and how to do so, debunking some of the myths that see the Green Witch as a predestined figure, who is already born a Witch and comes from a bloodline devoted to Witchcraft, and very often part of certain aesthetic, gender and propensity canons. In the next chapter we will introduce the magical garden, the power of possessing one's own to tend and cultivate. Infine we will show you the Wheel of the Year, the Witchcraft calendar-which deviates from the traditional calendar we are used to-with its holidays and celebrations.

Chapter 2

Grow Your Magic Garden

In this chapter, we will look at the benefits of owning your magical garden, how important it is to nurture your connection with Mother Earth, and how you can start creating your magical garden based on your needs and space. Don't worry: you don't have to have a large garden to start growing successfully. If you live in an apartment, there are several ways you can grow your magic garden using some tricks that we will look at in the next chapters. Growing your plants is an extraordinarily functional way to establish a bond of mutual fitness with them, which will come in handy when you use herbs, fires and essential oils in your recipes and spells. Next we will look in detail at the power of the seasons, what the Wheel of the Year is, and how the calendar traditional calendar differs from the Witch's calendar. You will learn what sabbats are and how you can celebrate and honor them by drawing on ancient traditions.

Pure Magic at Your Fingertips

Having one's magical garden is essential to a Green Witch's creative development. Caring for plants helps the Witch form a strong bond with them even before they are intended for their purpose-creating concoctions and potions that serve all the purposes of our vision. It would be great if everyone had large gardens to grow all kinds of plants, but modern life is often far removed from this ideal. If you live in a more rural area, in contact with pure nature, you can count yourself lucky. It is easier to connect with spontaneous nature, away from the influences of hectic city life. Unfortunately, however, this is often not possible. Many of us live in large cities, or even metropolises, where green spaces are small and limited to a few artificially created parks. Does this mean that this is bad? Absolutely not. The civilization to which we have arrived nowadays mirrors the needs that emerged in previous decades. Cities were formed in a certain way to be more comfortable and make us feel safer. Try to think of your ancestors, who lived in caves in the wilderness. Do you think they felt as safe as you feel in the comfort of your home? Certainly not. So don't see civilization as bad, but as a complement to wilderness. Both must coexist to maintain the balance and survival of each species.

Being a Green Witch means precisely understanding and accepting the duality of our world, and consciously deciding to be the mediator between these two sides, like a bridge connecting two islands in the middle of the ocean. Cultivating and growing your magical garden, whether small or large, helps you get to know your plants deeply and create an intense bond with them. A Green Witch not only uses plants and herbs to achieve her purposes, but also constantly communicates with them, draws energy and vitality from them, and contributes to the natural life cycle.

Many people have grown up with the idea that an ornamental plant is a mere decoration, or that a fruit plant serves only to produce food-nothing could be more wrong. First of all, a plant is a living thing. It breathes, it feeds, it emits vibrations. And, just like any living being, its well-being reflects the conditions in which it lives. A balanced, pacific and poised person transmits his inner serenity to his plants, which grow luxuriantly. In a chaotic environment, where there is high tension and malaise, a plant may, on the contrary, show signs of impatience even if it is exposed to sunlight and watered regularly. This is why, before you use plants for your recipes and potions, you must learn to understand and connect with plants in a deep way. A constant exchange of energy takes place between you and your plants, and affirm so that natural substances can thrive in your love and you can tap into their energy, respect and awareness is required.

How to Setup Your Magic Garden

Let's assume that no matter where you are, there will always be some type of plant that you will not be able to grow because of your geographic location, hours of sunshine, temperature, humidity, soil quality, and more. Therefore, especially if you are a beginner and do not possess a properly green thumb, a good tip to follow is, first and foremost, to understand what types of plants grow best in your area and in the environmental conditions that you can provide (sun, shade, half-shade, indoors, outdoors, cold greenhouse, etc.). Seeing your first seedlings grow thriving will provide you with the proper enthusiasm you need to face the little challenges you will encounter along the way.

You must know that your garden is alive, and like any living thing it can get sick or suffer accidents dictated by chance, for example hail, lack of sunshine, torrential rains, or attacks by pests, insects and other animals. If some things are not under your control, you can learn with experience to prevent or limit the damage by taking the proper steps.

Growing a plant, and, on a larger scale, a garden, requires a great deal of perseverance and patience. Nature knows exactly her times, and she will not change them because you are impatient or nervous. As you raise an animal or a child knowing that they enjoy their autonomy, you must do with plants. Your duties are few, albeit essential: ensure they get the right amount of light, water and nutrients from the soil, and protect them from environmental damage. Everything else is in nature's hands, perfect that way. But back to the environment: *how do you grow a garden indoors?* The options are many, depending on the type of house you live in.

The most logical place to think of is a balcony, porch or rooftop terrace. If you have one of these spaces, you have a huge advantage. All you need to do is get pots of different sizes, several dozen liters of soil and you're done. In winter, you could create a small greenhouse to grow your plants without worrying about them dying from frost. No balcony? Many plants, such as rosemary, sage and basil, live on the fine windowsill without any difficulty.

If, on the other hand, you don't own any outdoor space and your only available room is inside the house, don't despair. For many plants, the light that filters from a firewindow is sufficient. For example, if you live in an attic with skylights, you can think about dedicating a room (or part of a room) to your plants by noting where the sun lingers the longest. If, on the other hand, you have only classic fixtures, place your plants in the brightest spot in the house, next to the finest window that receives the most hours of sunlight; if necessary, remove the curtains to encourage the sun's rays to enter. But what to do when conditions in the house are less than optimal? Again, all is not lost. If you live in a house with particularly dry air, you will notice it by your plants' shriveled or rolled leaves. In this case you can buy a portable humidifier, small and handy, which will help increase the humidity in the air and consequently the well-being of your plants.

If not enough light enters your house, you may notice that your plants are discolored, tending to light yellow or even white, because they cannot absorb the amount of light needed to perform photosynthesis (which makes them green). What to do in this case? You can find grow lamps on the market: they are LED, consume little energy and help your plants grow well. A healthy plant is turgid, not affioshed, a nice bright green, with no dry or soft parts, and no white or black dots (which could be signs of infestation). If, on the other hand, you notice that your plants' leaves are turning dark brown, flosce, and the potting soil is always moist, it means there is too much moisture: in that case, reduce watering, or buy a dehumidifier to remove excessive moisture in the space.

The secret to a successful indoor garden is practicality. Depending on the space you can devote to plants, decide how many to buy, how to arrange them, and in which pots and containers. We generally tend to buy large pots thinking that the large amount of soil will help the plants grow bigger and stronger, but unfortunately the opposite is true. The pot should always be proportional to the size of the plant, and plants are usually repotted once or twice a year if the roots have taken up the whole pot. Smaller pots are also easier to move and relocate, especially if you anticipate a move soon. Putting different varieties of plants in the same pot is also a bad idea: sage and rosemary, for example, are natural antagonists and will tend to steal nutrients from each other, resulting in one plant perishing. Another possible drawback of putting different plants in the same pot is the spread of lice or other pests, which is why it is also a good idea to disinfect scissors every time you prune a plant. If you are not careful, from one diseased plant you may find your entire vegetable garden completely infested-we try to avoid that.

To give plants the best possible environment in which to grow, you need to opt for a draining soil, that is, one that does not retain excess water. To do this, it is sufficient to use a light soil and mix it with one-third perlite or expanded clay; it is also necessary for the pot to be perforated and possess its saucer (to collect the water that filters from the pot) or, if you do not like the pot-subpot combo, you can opt for a pot cover, that is, a closed pot that nevertheless serves as a pot cover as the plant is placed inside its "nursery pot" (the soft plastic pots in which the plants are sold). This way you will avoid water stagnation and ward off root rot that would lead to your plants dying. If you grow indoors, it is also important to fertilize the soil regularly. Fertilizing is also important outdoors, but it becomes much more necessary and frequent in places where the soil is confined inside a container. Choose a fertilizer of quality and according to your needs, avoiding "universal" fertilizers that often do not provide the right nutrients for plants.

Creating your first magic garden will not be difficult with these simple tips. However, only with experience will you fully understand your plants and figure out what is best for one and bad for the other. An interesting idea is to keep a small diary where you note the health status of your plants and how it changes with the seasons, fertilization and external factors. This way you will keep track of changes, what your plants prefer, and the types that live best in your environment. As mentioned at the beginning, if despite your best efforts some varieties of plants barely grow in your environment, don't blame yourself. You can give the plants to someone with an environment more conducive to growth. In Witch communities, exchanging plants and advice is not uncommon; it is a great way to meet other people and increase your knowledge.

The Power of Seasons

The essence of nature is represented by its cyclical nature. Days and nights follow one another, becoming weeks, months and seasons. As we all know, the solar year is divided into four seasons: winter, spring, summer and autumn. Each season has a different function and significance, which is why some Witches feel more affinity for one season than another. In Witchcraft, however, we do not see the four seasons as they are usually known. Ancient peoples had developed a real calendar, the Wheel of the Year, based mainly on seasonal cycles by observing the everlasting course of nature. To fully understand Witch Sabbaths, it is necessary to take a step back and discover how the circular idea of time was so important to the ancient pagans.

The seasonal cycles, dictated by Solstices and Equinoxes, had mainly a practical and vital function since Man's survival could depend on the proper preparation for these events. The Wheel of the Year, stylized as an 8-ray circle, has its roots through two natural cycles: the Sun's journey across the sky during the Solstices and Equinoxes and the seasonal cycle based on the harvest. The Witches' Sabbaths had mostly two major interpretations, both inescapable and intertwined in a perfect fusion. While the Sabbaths marked the most auspicious times for the harvest and well-being of the people, there was also a deep spiritual connection between Man and the nature that surrounded him and he experienced himself as an integral part of the Universe. The very presence of the divine was considered both creative and part of the Universe. Ancient civilizations have left us a tremendous legacy to enable us to understand the inestimable value of time, such as the testimony of the Stonehenge site: the accurate calculation of the passage of time and its associations to the stars were considered to all intents and purposes ritual codes, calculated so precisely as to establish an ever-deepening thread between Earth and Heaven. Not only did the Witches' Sabbaths represent the collaboration between Man and Nature, but they were also intense moments in which their magical-spiritual communion was celebrated.

Therefore, the Wheel of the Year represents the cyclical nature: *birth, death and rebirth*. Sabbats are related to solstices, equinoxes, and events between them. Sabbats are equally spaced on the calendar from each other. The four major sabbats are called Samhain (Oct. 31), Imbolc (Feb. 2), Beltane (May 1) and Lughnasadh (Aug. 1). They are also defined the *"Sabbats of the four met-*

ms," and indicate the beginning of the four seasons. The four minor Sabbats are Yule (Dec. 21), Litha (June 21), Ostara (March 21), and Mabon (Sept. 21), which correspond to the two equinoxes and two solstices. The 8 Witches' Sabbaths are moments of passage that mark the passage from one cycle to another, the beginning and end of critical and significant moments in the earthly and spiritual life of ancient and modern man. During these 8 Sacred Feasts, each witch's power reaches its peak and she can take advantage of the energy and magic that nature releases year after year. These days of reverence to one's Gods, unbridled celebration, feasting, recollection, introspection and revelry. Special moments when life and death are so close that they blur into each other. Let's see what the 8 Witches' Sabbaths are and what they represent.

Yule (December 21)

Yule signifies the winter solstice and is a festival of death, transformation and rebirth. It is a time laden with symbolic and magical values, as well as the time when the hours of daylight are the shortest of the year and, consequently, the hours of darkness are the longest. Nature at this time is in a state of dormancy to prepare to begin a new cycle, which is why human beings should also slow down and take a well-deserved break. Unfortunately, in the modern world, everything pushes in the opposite direction: this time of year, with the accumulation of celebrations and festivals, is a cause of stress. Finding a balance that allows for due rest in preparation for spiritual rebirth would be good. To celebrate Yule, you can get a large dry branch, paint it with gold paint and hang it outside the door of your home 9 days before the solstice, along with a marker and some strips of red paper to keep nearby. Anyone entering the house, if they wish, can write their wish on a strip of paper, which will be folded to ensure the secrecy of the wish and tied to the branch with a colored ribbon.

Imbolc (February 2)

Also called the Feast of the Crescent Moon, Imbolc brings grace, light and rebirth. The light born in Yule begins to manifest itself at the beginning of February: the days are gradually getting longer and, although the winter season continues to maintain its icy grip, something is changing. It is the time of renewal, of the earth's awakening, of hidden potential, and symbolizes hope because of this. To celebrate Imbolc you can light a white candle and meditate on the need for purification, to let go of things and aspects of your life that you no longer like, and the new things you want to bring into your existence.

Ostara (March 21)

Corresponding to the spring equinox, Ostara is the time of rebirth, change, fertility and sowing. Tradition has it that Witches lit fires at dawn to celebrate renewed life and for the protection of the harvest. To celebrate this holiday, you can decorate your house with field fires after thoroughly cleaning it. Spring cleaning, as it is sympathetically called, actually symbolizes the spiritual cleansing of the rooms. You can also create a floreal wreath to place in your hair and light green candles.

Beltane (May 1)

Midway between the spring equinox and the summer solstice, Beltane is the time of union and pleasure. It celebrates the return of the sun and the invigoration of the Earth. It is also a time of deep self-knowledge and personal growth. To celebrate Beltane, tradition calls for bathing in running wild waters as they are considered magical on the first morning of May. It is advisable in the last weeks of April to purify one's home with fumigations of juniper berries.

Litha (June 21)

It falls on the day of the summer solstice, the day with the most hours of daylight in the entire year. It is mistakenly considered the beginning of summer, but for the Wheel of the Year Litha marks the peak of summer, where magic reaches its maximum potential. Litha is the time for festivals, music, dancing and bonfires. Love and healing spells are most effective during this time of year. Bonfires are lit during Litha night, which in ancient times served to give light and ward off evil spirits. You can celebrate Litha by hanging a bunch of birch leaves, wild fennel, St. John's Wort and white lilac above your front door. If you can, light a bonfire of oak, fir and St. John's Wort outside, then skip it to propitiate good luck; alternatively, you can skip a lit red candle in the house. It is also said that buying garlic during Litha will give you a prosperous year.

Lughnasadh (August 1)

Also called Lammas, it is the day of the harvest festival. This day symbolizes the finish of the cycle of life (birth, growth and death to the finish of rebirth), for from a reaped ear of wheat (death) comes a seed that will give new life. The time has come to draw the first sums of the past year and reap the fruits planted and cultivated in us. Since it is a solar holiday, it is good to celebrate it in bright light, but if this is not feasible basterm light bonfires and candles so that the light shines even into the night. To celebrate Lughnasadh you can draw on an ancient tradition in which corn was used to create a doll that, kept fixed until the following year, had the power to appease a bountiful harvest in the future. Spells of abundance are favored at this time of year. To propitiate money and good fortune you can create a witch's bottle dedicated to the purpose.

Mabon (Semptember 21)

It corresponds to the autumn solstice and is celebrated to welcome the impending winter. During this time, animals prepare for hibernation and the world enters a state of peaceful rest. It is considered a time of balance, where one can slow down the pace and enjoy the fruits of one's labor. Unfinished projects can be completed in anticipation of the arrival of that part of the year when it is good to leave the outside to explore one's inner self. Protection spells are most efficient at this time of year. To celebrate Mabon you can create a table centerpiece with dried flowers and herbs (fresh ones are not suitable at this time of year), such as chestnuts, pinecones, sage and autumn leaves. Tradition dictates that you light a bonfire with dried leaves from your garden; if that is not possible, just light a brown candle.

Samhain (October 31)

Also known as the Celtic New Year, Samhain is the threshold toward the finish of the cycle. Nature gives the last fruits before going into rest. It is a time for meditation, calm, and waiting; propitious for learning divinatory techniques, such as tarot cards or runes, and reflecting on what has been and will bem. A powerful practice to do on this occasion is decluttering: letting go of everything that no longer makes us feel good or vibrates at the same frequency. If these are feelings, you can write them down on slips of paper, which you then burn with the flame of a black candle.

Final Thoughts

In this chapter we discovered the powers and benefits of owning a magical garden, how cultivation can help build a lasting bond with plants and enhance the Witch's experience and connection with nature. You learned to create your magical garden from scratch, regardless of your space and green thumb. We saw that it is not necessary to own large plots of land and open spaces to bring our garden to life, but that even a bright corner of the house can serve the purpose well. We addressed the issues most common to garden lovers: moisture, soil, light and pests. Finally, we learned about the power of the seasons, the composition of the Wheel of the Year, pagan holidays and what you can do to honor them. By the end of this chapter, you should feel ready to tackle the next one and begin navigating the sea of potion making and herbal recipes.

Chapter 3
Herbs & Magical Recipes

In Green Magic, the undisputed stars of recipes and rituals are, of course, plants. In Witchcraft, many other ingredients are used, both of animal, plant and inorganic origin such as stones, ribbons, pins, hair, nails, blood, wine, seals, photographs, and more, which help to strengthen spells and rituals. Before using any herb, it is best to know and ascertain its properties and wholesomeness, as well as the safe ways to use it. Some plants may be toxic for internal use but not for external use, or vice versa; they may be beneficial in oleol form but toxic if you inhale fumigations of them. In any case, before you act, inform yourself thoroughly and make sure you are not endangering yourself or others. This also applies to allergies or intolerances of yourself and those around you.

Beware: at one time witches used to use even poisonous herbs in their concoctions to induce confusional states and ecstasies and prophetic visions and clairvoyance. This chapter will list the main poisonous herbs and how they were used. Under no circumstances will you ever be suggested to ingest such substances or inspire fumigations produced by these plants. Toxic plants should be handled with extreme caution and out of the reach of animals, children and unsuspecting people. Tradition dictates that the herbs used by Witches are collected personally. Still, since not all herbs are readily available and not everyone has the right knowledge to recognize them, it is always best to obtain supplies from your trusted herbalist when in doubt. The herbalist's herbs are certified, so they are safe to use.

Gathering & storing herbs

Whether you gather them from your garden or in the woods and open country, there are many aspects to consider before harvesting a plant. First of all, it is always wise to keep an eye on your larder of ingredients and avoid harvesting flowers and herbs you already possess enough of. Ingredients do not always keep at their best and for a long time despite our care and attention, so picking plants that we do not need immediately could turn into a waste, should you have to throw them away. Another important aspect is to be clear about what you need. Only a certain part of a plant may be required in a recipe: leaves, roots, petals, pistils, bark, buds, and more. You should never harvest the entire plant by tearing it out of the ground: many parts may be useless to you and be thrown in the trash. If you need the petals of a flower, cut off only the affected part and be sure to leave the plant's mother in good health, heal the wound and continue to live.

If you pick herbs and flowers in the woods or non-private areas, make sure they are not protected plants, the picking of which could bring you trouble from forest rangers. Also find out if there are quantity limits on collecting a certain plant. Better avoid fines and reports by informing yourself about what you can and cannot do on public lands. Once you have collected the herbs you need, you need to decide whether to use them fresh or preserve them by drying. Before drying anything make sure to clear it of soil, dust and insects. You can dry the plants in the sun, or by hanging them in bunches in a dry, clean area of the house. It is important that you leave the plants exposed only long enough for them to dry, otherwise they will gather dust and, as a result, may become unusable. Many people leave herbs to dry in the kitchen, near the cooking area, because the air is usually less humid than in the rest of the house, but this is a bad idea: the grease that evaporates during the cooking of food gets deposited on all surfaces (just keep an eye on the filters of the extractor hood once a week to realize this), greasing even the herbs hanging to dry.

For this reason, the kitchen should be avoided unless you own a spacious room or open space. If you do not have the patience to let the herbs dry naturally, you can opt for a dryer or to dry the herbs in an oven at a medium temperature with the door half-open to let the moisture escape. As is the case with storing witch bottles, the best containers for storing your herbs for a long time are opaque or, better yet, amber glass containers with a cork stopper and a label to write the contents. It is important to label each jar to avoid confusing ingredients and compromising your spell recipes.

The Witch's Herbarium

A

Acacia: protection from negative influences.

Aloe: protection, good luck.

Ambrosia: courage.

Anise: protection, youth, purification.

Ash: healing, health.

B

Bamboo: occult protection, good luck.

Basil: protection, health, exorcism.

Burdock: healing, protection.

Belladonna: visions, astral projections (POISONOUS)

Beech: creativity, making dreams come true.

Benzoin: sensitivity, optimism, financial prosperity.

Bergamot: money.

Birch: protection, exorcism.

Blueberry: protection, luck, magical dreams, breaking curses.

Blackberry: healing, money, protection, strength.

C

Cactus: chastity, protection.

Catnip: love, happiness, beauty.

Calamus: luck, wealth, protection.

Camellia: wealth.

Chamomile: sleep, love, money.

Camphor: divination.

Cinnamon: spirituality, success, love, strength.

Carrot: fertility.

Caraway: protection against theft, health.

Cascara Sagrada: resolution of legal issues, protection, money.

Cedar: healing, purification, protection.

Cypress: healing, exorcism.

Coriander: love, aphrodisiac.

Chasteberry: relaxation.

D

Dandelion: divination, wish fulfillment.

Dicentra: love.

Digital purpurea: protection (POISONOUS)

Dionea: love, protection.

Devil's claw: love, occult protection.

E

Elderberry: protection, sleep, prosperity, healing.

Eucalyptus: protection, healing.

Euphorbia: purification, protection.

F

Fern: clairvoyance, fertility.

Figs: divination, love, fertility.

G

Galanga: luck, love, long life.

Garlic: protection, healing, aphrodisiac.

Galbanum: vitality, occult protection.

Gardenia: healing, love, spirituality.

Gentian: occult protection.

Geranium: fertility, love.

Ginger: success, love, money

H

Hawthorn: fertility, protection of children.

Hazel: luck, fertility, protection, wishes.

Holly: protection, luck, magical dreams.

Holy thistle: strength, protection.

Hellebore: exorcism, astral travel.

Heather: good luck, keeping spirits and goblins away.

Hyssop: purification, against the evil eye.

Hypericum: protection from demons, good luck charm.

I

Iris: divination, spiritual healing.

Ivy: healing, protection.

J

Jasmine: prosperity, money.

Juniper: exorcism, protection from thieves.

K

Kava-kava: visions, astral projection.

L

Lavender: love, protection, sleep, chastitm, purification, peace, long life.

Laurel: success, energy, purification.

Licorice: lust, love, fidelity.

Lilac: exorcism, protection.

Lime tree: joy, luck, happiness.

M

Magnolia: fidelity.

Mallow: love, protection.

Mandrake: protection, fertility, money, love, health.

Mugwort: purification, protection.

Mistletoe: love, fertility, health.

Myrrh: protection, exorcism, healing, spirituality.

N

Narcissus: love, fertility, luck.

Nettle: protection, healing.

Nutmeg: luck, money, health, fidelity.

O

Oak: protection, health, healing, power.

Orange blossom: love, calm, health.

Olive: healing, peace, fertility, lust.

Olive tree: healing, peace, protection.

Orchid: love.

P

Poppy: fertility, love, sleep, luck.

Patchouli: money, fertility, lust.

Pepper: protection, exorcism.

Peppermint: purification, sleep, love, healing, psychic powers.

Peach: love, fertility, longevity.

Pine: healing protection, money.

Parsley: purification, protection, lust.

R

Raspberry: protection, love.

Rhubarb: protection, faithfulness.

Rose: love, psychic powers, healing, divination for love, luck in love, protection.

Rosemary: protection, purification, acceptance.

Rue: healing, health, mental powers, love.

S

Sage: immortality, longevity, wisdom, protection.

Saffron: lust, strength.

Sandalwood: protection, wish fulfillment, healing, spirituality.

Strawberry: love, luck.

T

Thyme: purification, psychic powers, sleep.

V

Valerian: love, sleep, protection.

Vanilla: love, lust, psychic powers.

Verbena: peace, money, youth.

Viburnum: protection from evil spirits.

Violet: lust, desires, peace, healing.

W

Wild bergamot: clarity, lucidity.

Y

Yarrow: courage, love, psychic powers, exorcism

Herbarium of poisonous herbs

Since ancient times, witches have developed a deep knowledge of plants and their properties, both beneficial and toxic. Specific plants with poisonous components were used for specific purposes, such as provoking visions, astral travel, prophecies and mystical experiences, or to symbolically "poison" adversity through bottles of protection against the evil eye or otherwise. For example, alkaloids contained in some plants, which are nothing more than substances secreted by plants to defend themselves, were used to induce deep trance states. Since the plants listed below are highly toxic, their use is not recommended for those unfamiliar with handling poisonous substances or if there is a risk of these plants being accidentally ingested by animals and children.

Aconitum

The genus name, Aconitum, comes from the Greek akòniton, which literally means "poisonous plant." It is associated with Saturn, the water element and the female gender. According to tradition, its powers are protection and invisibility. It is a wild plant, growing mainly on escarpments, and its flower is a fascinating purplish blue. The alkaloids in this plant are effective even if only by contact, being toxic on the skin, but they are mostly concentrated in the roots, which is why it is difficult to poison yourself by accident. The poison must be extracted through the roots and in ancient times was used to anoint the tips of arrows and spears. The aconite poison leads to respiratory and cardiac paralysis, killing humans and animals within minutes. Wolfsbane is also called "wolfsbane" and is said to keep vampires and werewolves away.

Belladonna

Belladonna enjoys the title of the most poisonous common plant currently known. The name derives from the fact that this was once used in cosmetics. Women used belladonna as eye drops to make their eyes languid, as the alkaloids paralyzed the pupil, making it larger. Of course, the practice was extremely dangerous, especially if continued, as prolonged use would damage eyesight. It is a wild plant that grows in mountainous territories, around 1,400 meters above sea level and shady areas. It possesses reddish-brown fires from which sprout red berries that turn black and glossy as they ripen, similar to a blueberry. Ingestion of a single berry can potentially kill a child. It used to treat stomach and intestinal cramps, or as an anesthetic, finally discovered that the cause of countless patient deaths was belladonna itself.

Hemlock

As history tells us, hemlock was used to poison enemies and eliminate inconvenient individuals. Socrates was sentenced to death through a concoction containing hemlock because he was accused of denying the existence of the gods. In appearance it is very similar to wild carrot and wild parsley, both in foliage and flowers. This is why it is highly advisable not to harvest wild carrots and parsley, which, in any case, lack the taste and scent of cultivated ones. Over the centuries, this poisonous plant has become a symbol of betrayal. It was much used in court intrigues and royal disputes: it was enough to make the person concerned drink hemlock in the form of an herbal tea to get rid of it for good. In small doses it was used as a sedative, antispasmodic, and analgesic, seriously endangering the lives of those who consumed it.

Black hellebore

Black hellebore is the most common variant of the Helleborus, which has more than thirty species. It is also called the "Christmas rose" because it is one of the few plants whose fires bloom in midwinter, and it is a spontaneous perennial plant that grows in moist soils, at the edge of hilly forests, and in cool, shady areas. All parts of the plant, including the roots, are toxic and highly irritating to humans and animals. We have traces of the use of black hellebore as a remedy for mental illness as far back as Ancient Greece. Mythology relates that Heracles (Hercules) was cured of insanity by this very plant. For the Greeks, the expression "you need hellebore" was equivalent to our modern "you need a shrink," meaning it was a way of calling someone crazy. Over the centuries, hellebore has also been used in exorcisms to induce astral travel. In Wicca it is used to ward off evil spirits. Hellebore is deadly only in large quantities, while in small amounts it is still used in medicine as a cardiotonic and purgative. Although it is not deadly in small doses, its use for home remedies is not recommended.

Henbane

Henbane is a widespread species throughout Europe, where it grows wild in neglected areas, along roadsides and in nitrate-rich soils. Its fires consist of five yellow petals with a distinctive purple reticulation, as are the purple corolla and pistils. In this plant, the highest concentration of alkaloids is found in the leaves, which are toothed and flaccid. In the past it was used by witches and shamans to induce hallucinations, trance states and clairvoyance. In folk medicine it was used as an antispasmodic and to treat asthma. When taken in small doses, henbane is not lethal, although side effects such as tachycardia, dry mucous membranes, hallucinations, and delusional states may be experienced. In large doses it can lead to coma and even death.

Mandrake

Mandrake is among the most famous magical plants in popular culture, present in modern legends and stories that, albeit revisited, contribute to the popularity of this plant with countless uses. It is a toxic plant whose roots have an anthropomorphic appearance, that is, they resemble the shape of the human body. Since ancient times it was believed to be a plant with powerful magical properties, to be used either by ingestion or as an amulet. Its root was believed to cure infertility and insomnia, protect against disease, and even attract love with its aphrodisiac properties. It was also used in exorcisms because evil spirits are said to flee from this root. Even in Ancient Greece it was customary to keep a mandrake root near the bed as its smell promoted sleep. In large amounts it can cause hallucinations, vomiting, tachycardia, high blood pressure, convulsions and even death.

Stramonium

Because of its high concentration of alkaloids, stramonium is also called "devil's weed." Its active ingredients act directly on the nervous and cardiovascular systems, causing serious problems for those who ingest it.

It possesses very pretty, bell-shaped, white flowers. In ancient times, stramonium was mainly used as a narcotic, to neutralize victims or to cause hallucinations in them. On the other hand, medical use was quite rare, limited to the purpose of a muscle relaxant. Shamans and sorceresses extensively used it in small quantities to induce hallucinations and states of spiritual enlightenment.

The 15 Essential Herbs for Witches

Although witches use various herbs and plants to create remedies and potions, a short list of medicinal herbs can be considered the go-tos of every Green Witch. The reason for the preferential use of the use of these particular herbs is partly due to the ease of availability and cost of purchase (in case one goes to an herbalist), but also and especially because these herbs, more than others, have properties that can benefit a wide variety of purposes. In this section we will look together at the 15 most commonly used medicinal herbs by witches and find out their benefits and purposes in detail.

Laurel

Gender: Male

Planet: Sun

Element: Fire

Therapeutic properties: digestive, diuretic, expectorant

Magical properties: protection, psychic powers, healing, purification, strength

Historical background: Apollo's priestesses used to chew laurel leaves and inhale their fumigations to induce a state of higher enlightenment. For both Romans and Greeks, laurel symbolized victory, and thus superiority over others. That is why it was used to adorn the heads of the most distinguished people worthy of the highest honor.

Description: Laurel is a perennial evergreen plant belonging to the Lauraceae family and is widespread in the Mediterranean basin. Its size is around 4-5 meters, but it is not uncommon to find specimens reaching 10 meters in height. It tolerates pruning well, so it is possible to keep laurel small even in smaller gardens. It can also be grown in pots, as long as it has plenty of sunlight. Laurel is used in cooking to flavor dishes, as bay leaves possess a very strong and distinctive scent and flavor.

Uses in Witchcraft: Laurel is used in magic primarily for its protective qualities and clairvoyance. Keeping a laurel leaf under the pillow promotes prophetic dreams and protects against negative energies and the evil eye. Laurel trees protect surrounding properties from evil. When burned together with sandalwood, laurel removes curses and black magic spells.

Mugwort

Gender: Female

Planet: Venus

Element: Earth

Therapeutic properties: sedative, antispasmodic, antiseptic, digestive

Magical properties: strength, psychic powers, healing, astral projections and prophetic dreams

Historical background: It is said to be named for Artemis, the Greek goddess of hunting. In Greek mythology, the plant was considered a symbol of women and fertility. It was customary to leave a few bunches hanging in the house to ward off evil spirits. Mugwort is even mentioned in the Bible for its therapeutic properties.

Description: Mugwort is a perennial plant belonging to the Asteraceae family, from which the famous Absinthe is produced: a distillate with a controversial reputation. The mugwort plant is a medium-sized shrub, with an average height of one meter, and its fiers are yellow and arranged in clusters.

Uses in Witchcraft: Keeping mugwort under the pillow promotes prophetic dreams and astral projections. A mugwort leaf in shoes gives strength and willpower to embark on new and long journeys, or face a competition involving intensive use of the legs and feet. When passed over doors and fixtures, Mugwort essential oil keeps away elves and evil spirits.

Basil

Gender: Male

Planet: Mars

Element: Fire

Therapeutic properties: antispasmodic, diuretic, vermifuge, sleep, anti-vertigo

Magical properties: love, wealth, protection, exorcism

Historical background: Its name comes from the Greek word basileus meaning "king." Not surprisingly, in Latin we referred to what is royal with the term basilicum. To the Romans it was considered a sacred plant with magical properties. It was customary to place a basil leaf on the heart of deceased rulers to assure them of opening the gates to the Afterlife.

Description: Basil includes approximately 40 different varieties. Some of the more unusual types we know are Indian and red basil. Traditional basil, the one we all know and use, is a plant that reaches 30-40 centimeters in height and has elongated oval leaves that are bright green. At the end of the season it fills with pretty little white fillings, from which basil seeds are obtained. In all homes, basil is used to flavor dishes or to decorate them. An aromatic herb can give off an intense, enveloping scent as soon as you brush its leaves. But in addition to its use in cooking, basil has countless beneficial properties.

Uses in Witchcraft: witches make extensive use of basil in potions, pouches, witch bottles, infusions, decoctions, and more. When placed near the house's front door, it is used in protection spells and a negativity repellent. It is also employed to appease the arrival of money, so you can place a basil leaf in your wallet or in the cash recorder of your business to promote higher profits.

Chamomille

Gender: Male

Planet: Sun

Element: Water

Therapeutic properties: antimicrobial, antiseptic, antibacterial, antinflammatory, carminative, spasmolytic, healing.

Magical properties: money, love, protection Historical background: Discovered by the Egyptians around 1500 B.C., chamomile was initially used as a remedy for fever and as a skin soother. According to the Egyptians, the fire of chamomile was reminiscent of the sun, so they consecrated chamomile to the god Ra. Later, medieval monks discovered the immense qualities of chamomile after discovering that if planted near a diseased tree, it was able to make it heal.

Description: Chamomile is an annual herbaceous plant belonging to the Asteraceae family. It has a slender stem between 15 and 50 centimeters in height on top of which is a single inflorescence with a yellow corolla and white petals. It is mainly used in infusions and decoctions to conciliate sleep and calm the body and mind. It is also highly used in cosmetics, soothing creams, or lightening hair. Chamomile decoctions are also very effective for soothing reddened skin and relieving swelling and burning in the eyes.

Uses in Witchcraft: the use of chamomile in witchcraft harkens back to its therapeutic properties translated to a spiritual plane. It is used as a soother for the spirit, to soothe emotional wounds, to quiet the mind, and to attract money when added to witchcraft pouches and bottles. It is also an excellent protector: scattering dried chamomile flowers in the house's four corners cancels curses and spells against those living there.

Cinnamon

Gender: Male

Planet: Sun

Element: Fire

Therapeutic properties: antiseptic, eupeptic, gastrointestinal spasms,

Magical properties: spirituality, success, love, strength.

Historical background: Cinnamon is among the oldest spices used in cooking today. Although it originated in Sri Lanka, its intense fragrance and therapeutic power won over nobles and aristocrats worldwide, so much so that it earned the title "spice of kings." The Egyptians have used it in embalming since 2000 B.C., but we know that in 2700 B.C. this spice was already widely used in China in the medical field. Cinnamon is also mentioned in the Bible, when God commands Moses to consecrate the Temple with a mixture of aromatic substances. There is also a legend about cinnamon handed down by Greek and Roman historians that a bird called cinnamologus built its nests from cinnamon sticks.

Description: Cinnamon is a spice native to Sri Lanka made from the inner bark of the cinnamon tree, a member of the Lauraceae family. The cinnamon tree measures approximately 10 to 15 meters and is evergreen. The flavor and scent of cinnamon are unmistakable, although they are vaguely reminiscent of those of cloves. In cooking it is used extensively to impart a distinctive, spicy flavor to herbal teas and sweets. Eastern and Creole tradition also employs it in savory, accompanying smoked and unsmoked meats.

Uses in Witchcraft: When burned as incense, cinnamon can raise magical vibrations, stimulate psychic powers and produce protective vibrations. When brought on in witch's pouches or bottles it promotes sexual attraction and increased libido.

Jasmine

Gender: Female

Planet: Moon Element: Water

Therapeutic properties: anti-stress, antioxidant

Magical properties: love, money, prophetic dreams, protection from evil spirits

Historical background: Jasmine is a fire related to esoterism since ancient times, known as an amulet of protection. Fragments of jasmine petals have been found in the grave goods of pharaohs' tombs. An all-Italian legend tells that Cosimo de Medici was the first to cultivate jasmine on the Italic peninsula and forbade its spread outside the land he owned. However, a young gardener stole a jasmine plant to give to his beloved, who planted it in the ground. It is said that the plant had an enviable bloom, and from that seedling stolen from de Medici sprang all the jasmine plants that spread throughout Tuscany. Legend has it that the two young lovers married and lived their lives together, united and happy. Since that day, jasmine has been a symbol of unity and happiness, so much so that even today, in Tuscany, brides have a jasmine branch added to their wedding bouquet as a good omen.

Description: Jasmine is a vigorous climbing plant belonging to the Apocynaceae family that can reach 4 meters in height. Its flowers can be white, yellow or soft pink. Native to the Himalayan slopes, the Egyptians used it to scent bath water and statues of the gods, while in the East it was used to flavor black tea, reserved for emperors. One of the best known methods of consuming jasmine today is through tea, which is still very popular among Orientals. The aroma of jasmine is sought after, and today it is used in the creation of sweets, while in the past it was very present in food generally on the tables of nobles.

Uses in Witchcraft: Green Witches are wont to include jasmine flowers in infusions and decoctions that propitiate love. When worn, jasmine []re attracts wealth and prosperity. A bunch of fresh jasmines on the bedside table helps to conciliate sleep and induce prophetic dreams.

St. John's Wort

Gender: Male

Planet: Mars

Element: fire

Therapeutic properties: anti-inflammatory, healing, antidepressant, anxiolytic.

Magical properties: love, money, protection, success, happiness.

Historical background: this plant is named after John the Baptist because it blooms around August 29, the date of the saint's beheading. For more than 2,000 years it has been used primarily as a healing agent. The Greeks and Romans believed St. John's Wort effectively against witch spells. On the other hand, Christians thought the plant could ward off evil spirits, and on St. John's Day they burned St. John's Wort in large bonfires to purify the air, drive away evil spirits and propitiate good harvests. When the first settlers introduced St. John's Wort to North America, it was discovered that the Indigenous people were already making recurring use of it, with purposes similar to those in Europe.

Description: St. John's Wort is a perennial plant in the Clusiaceae family that can reach 40 centimeters in height. It is a hardy plant that grows along roadsides and in uncultivated fields and is particularly weedy if not kept at bay with frequent pruning. Hypericum flowers are bright yellow and have a very delicate appearance. In fitotherapy, St. John's Wort is mainly used as an oleolyte or ointment because of its antiseptic, healing, astringent, purifying, emollient and soothing properties.

Uses in Witchcraft: witches used St. John's Wort in their oleolites to soothe the skin and in infusions to combat coughs, catarrh, colds and urinary tract inflammation. Putting St. John's Wort root in a small bag brings money and riches. Greasing household doors and fixtures with St. John's Wort oil helps keep disease away.

Lavender

Gender: Female

Planet: Mercury

Element: Air

Therapeutic properties: analgesic, antibacterial, sedative, hypotensive.

Magical properties: love, protection, sleep, chastity, purification, peace, long life.

Historical background: The term "lavender" comes from the Latin gerund of the verb "to wash" because of its use to cleanse and purify the body. The ancient Greeks are thought to have referred to lavender as "Nard," which is also echoed in the Bible. The Egyptians used to use lavender as an ingredient in their body ointments and also in oil lamps. In medieval times lavender was used to drive away witches and protect against demons. Lavender's scientific name, "Lavandula," was given in the 17th century by the French botanist Joseph Pitton de Tournefort.

Description: Lavender is a shrubby and hardy plant belonging to the Lamiaceae family. It is used to grow in dry soils and has a bushy habit. Lavender stems can be up to two meters tall, and the spike-shaped inflorescence is purple or deep pink and very aromatic.

Uses in Witchcraft: Lavender is used in magic for multiple purposes. One of the main ones is love: rubbing lavender oil on the body will propitiate love, while keeping a sprig of lavender in your pocket will protect you from abusive partners. The scent of lavender is an elixir of youth: smelling it lengthens life and dissolves negative thoughts. Because of its purifying and antibacterial power, lavender is often used in purifying baths before a ritual.

Mint

Gender: Male

Planet: Mercury

Element: Air

Therapeutic properties: anesthetic, analgesic, decongestant.

Magical properties: purification, sleep, love, healing, psychic powers, lust.

Historical background: Greek mythology links the name of this herb to that of the nymph Mint, a creature of extraordinary beauty. According to legend, the nymph was transformed into the mint plant by Persephone, the jealous wife of Hades whose concubine Mint was, and her mentholated perfume was given to him by the god of the Underworld as a final gesture of love. Mint was highly valued in antiquity for its therapeutic and flavoring qualities. The Bible tells us that the Hebrews used it to perfume and uplift the spirit, while the Greeks and Romans valued this herb as a sexual stimulant, to the point that newlywed brides inserted sprigs of mint in their wedding crowns in the hope of being pleasing to their husbands.

Description: Mint is a plant part of the Lamiaceae family, to which lavender also belongs. It is strongly aromatic, with a typically pungent and spicy odor. The plant is generally perennial in cycle and can reach five feet in height.

Mint is mainly used to flavor dishes and beverages, especially alcoholic cocktails because its intense, fresh flavor mitigates alcohol. It can also be used alone in infusions and decoctions, excellent for a balsamic and decongestant effect.

Uses in Witchcraft: Fresh peppermint is placed on the altar to summon good spirits. It is especially good in spells and recipes that attract large sums of money. When used in oil, mint can be used as a body scent to seduce your partner.

Rose

Gender: Female

Planet: Venus

Element: Water

Therapeutic properties: soothing, anti-wrinkle, anti-inflammatory.

Magical properties: love, psychic powers, healing, divination for love, luck in love, protection.

Historical background: The rose has been among the best known and most cultivated flowers since ancient times. Of the original 150 species, we now count more than 2,000. We have evidence of rose cultivation from all over the Mediterranean basin. In ancient times it was grown not only for ornamental purposes, but also to extract its essential oil. The origins of the rose are intertwined with the myth of Adonis and Aphrodite. According to legend, when a wild boar attack mortally wounded Adonis, Aphrodite ran to his rescue, but injured herself with brambles. From the blood gushing from his wounds bloomed beautiful red roses. The goddess could do nothing to save Adonis, but Zeus, pitying the goddess' pain, allowed Adonis to return for four months of the year to the realm of the living to be with his beloved. From this legend we grasp why red roses have always been attributed the meaning of deep love, capable of defeating even death.

Description: There are more than two thousand known species of roses. The genus "rose" includes bushy, sarmentose, climbing, creeping, shrub and sapling species, and more. Of the original 150, only 30 are wild species. The colors of roses available today are almost endless and can meet anyone's needs. The rose remains one of the most prized flowers of all time and, depending on its color, takes on special significance.

However, the rose is not only employed as a decorative element. Rose petals are highly used in cosmetics to create soothing products such as creams, oils, and rose water. There is also quite widespread use of roses as a culinary ingredient.

Uses in Witchcraft: Always a quintessential sign of love, the rose in Witchcraft is mainly used for love strains, spells, and Red Magic potions. Although the choice of the Rose's color determines its meaning, in general roses signify love in all its forms, even friendly, brotherly and platonic. Roses planted in the garden attract fairies, while a tea of rosebuds promotes prophetic dreams.

Rosemary

Gender: Male

Planet: Sun

Element: Fire

Therapeutic properties: antiemetic, antirheumatic.

Magical properties: protection, purification, acceptance.

Historical background: Ancient peoples considered rosemary a plant with exceptional therapeutic and aromatic properties. The Romans made rosemary a symbol of death and love, and they burned sprigs of rosemary during sacrifices in honor of their gods. Rosemary was considered an aphrodisiac, which if taken in large doses could cause abortion. It was also used to take baths aimed at stimulating blood circulation.

Description: Rosemary is a shrubby evergreen plant in the Lamiaceae family that can reach fix to 3 meters in height. The stems are woody and brown, while the twigs are light green. It is a plant that can grow easily without any special care, withstand long periods of drought, but does not tolerate cold temperatures well if prolonged. Besides as an aromatic herb used in cooking, rosemary is used in cosmetics for shampoos and other hair products, as well as for the production of monofloral honey since bees are fond of rosemary flowers.

Uses in Witchcraft: rosemary has high purifying properties, so witches have it burned as incense to eliminate negativity. A sprig of rosemary under the pillow comforts sleep and keeps nightmares away. Hanging a rosemary wreath above the front door keeps burglars away.

Sage

Gender: Male

Planet: Jupiter

Element: Air

Therapeutic properties: antiseptic, carminative, astringent, antisudorific

Magical properties: immortality, longevity, wisdom, protection.

Historical background: Greeks and Romans called it "the herb of health," and its harvesting was reserved for a chosen few who had to be categorically dressed in white and barefoot. A plant of shamans par excellence was used to ward off evil spirits and purify the air. In the Middle Ages it took hold instead as a healing agent. In the 17th century, a basket and of sage was exchanged by Dutch merchants for three baskets of tea because of how valuable it was.

Description: Sage, which owes its name to its ability to "save life," is a genus of plants belonging to the Lamiaceae family. The peculiar shape of its leaves and its characteristic roughness make it resemble a tongue. This has contributed, over the years, to its gaining popularity as a natural remedy for mouth and tooth care. Its main use is in cooking, either as a flavoring for meats and vegetables or as a side dish.

Uses in Witchcraft: sage is the symbol of wisdom. It is used in spells and potions to promote knowledge, but also to promote money and health. It is said that planting sage alone in one's garden brings bad luck, so it is advisable to have a stranger plant it.

Dandelion

Gender: Male

Planet: Jupiter

Element: Air

Therapeutic properties: digestive, choleretic, depurative and diuretic

Magical properties: Divination, wishes, calling of spirits

Historical background: Dandelion, was already in use in 10th century Arabia. Physicians prescribed dandelion to purify the blood. By the sixteenth century, a real therapeutic fad broke out with dandelion, which seemed to be able to cure all ills.

Description: Dandelion is a wild, sometimes weedy herbaceous plant that grows in meadows and wetlands. The plant averages between 10 and 30 centimeters in height, with broad toothed leaves and a yellow fibre from which forms the inflorescence that we all enjoyed blowing. Dandelion is used both in cooking and in natural leaf or root therapies. Loved by bees, dandelion is useful for creating monofloreal honey. One of the most popular homemade recipes in traditional cooking is non-dandelion honey, also called dandelion syrup-a vegan and tasty alternative to honey, made only with dandelion flowers and sugar.

Uses in Witchcraft: Dandelion dried root is used to prepare infusions that accentuate psychic powers. Burning dried dandelion fires as an incense summons spirits.

Thyme

Gender: Female

Planet: Venus

Element: Water

Therapeutic properties: antimicrobial, antispasmodic.

Magical properties: health, sleep, psychic powers, courage, love, purification.

Historical background: Thyme enjoyed great fame even in ancient times. The Egyptians used thyme for embalming processes, while the Greeks used it in food. In the Middle Ages, on the other hand, it was used as a nightmare dispeller: a sprig under the pillow ensured peaceful sleep. As a superstition, soldiers would have a sprig of thyme painted on their shield by their consorts.

Description: Thyme, which like lavender, sage and rosemary is a member of the Lamiaceae family, is a genus of plants whose name means "strength" and "courage," because of the sensation its aromatic scent instills when sniffed. It is a shrubby plant that can reach 50 centimeters in height and is aesthetically reminiscent of rosemary. Thyme decoctions are an effective remedy for treating urinary tract and respiratory infections, while thyme oil reduces persistent headaches.

Uses in Witchcraft: It is widely used in healing spells because of its antimicrobial and antiseptic properties. A sprig of thyme under the pillow keeps nightmares away and promotes restful sleep.

Verbena

Gender: Female

Planet: Moon

Element: Water

Therapeutic properties: disinfectant, healing, digestive.

Magical properties: protection, love, purification, youthfulness

Historical background: The Romans considered verbena a sacred plant with magical properties, and used it to adorn temples and statues of deities, and to clean Jupiter's altars.

Description: Verbena is a perennial, wild plant in the verbenaceae family. Its maximum height is about 80 centimeters. Its flowers are usually a beautiful deep pink that lightens toward the outside of the petals, but orange, red and dark purple varieties can be found. As an herbal remedy, it is recommended to be taken as a decoction to combat various ailments and decongest the respiratory tract.

Uses in Witchcraft: Dried verbena, sprinkled throughout the home, brings serenity and peace. Every part of the plant enjoys protective power so that you can create protective amulets with any part obtained from verbena.

Enchant your herbs

Before herbs are used in recipes and rituals, they must be enchanted to align the plant's vibrations with the intention and purpose for which you want to use them. It is not necessary to enchant one herb at a time if you need several for your purpose; the important thing is that the energetically charged herbs be used as soon as possible, otherwise the enchantment will weaken and will not have the effect you expect.

To charge the herbs you need to settle down in a comfortable and quiet place, away from possible distractions and interruptions. Sit on the floor cross-legged and spend a few minutes meditating to clarify your intent within yourself. If you like, you can light an incense. Once you feel aligned with your intent, clasp the herbs to be charged in your hands and, with your eyes closed, visualize transferring the energy of intention to the herbs through your palms. Keep focusing on your goal until you feel you have infused sufficient energy into the herbs. You have now enchanted your herbs, which are ready to be used.

Chapter 4

Magical Infusions

Warning: before consuming any of these recipes, seek advice from your health care provider. You may be allergic or sensitive to any of the ingredients in the recipes, or may have picked a plant wrong. The author assumes no responsibility for careless consumption of the recipes listed below.

To Manifest Prosperity

Ingredients:

- One teaspoon of dried jasmine.
- One teaspoon of dried mint
- One teaspoon of melissa officinalis
- Two teaspoons of honey

Procedure:

1. Make 500 ml of water to heat.
2. Once hot, remove from heat and pour in all ingredients.
3. Let stand 10 minutes, then serve.

To Attract Money

Ingredients:

- One teaspoon of dioecious pimenta.
- One teaspoon of dried chamomile flowers
- Five to six dried blackberries
- Two teaspoons of honey

Procedure:

1. Make 500 ml of water to heat.
2. Once hot, remove from heat and pour in all ingredients.
3. Let it rest 10 minutes, then serve.

To Attract True Love

Ingredients:

- Three rose or red rose petals from organic cultivation (no pesticides).
- Half teaspoon of cinnamon powder.
- Two dried strawberries
- Four dried raspberries
- Two teaspoons of sugar

Procedure:

1. Make 500 ml of water to heat.
2. Once hot, remove from heat and pour in all ingredients.
3. Let it rest 10 minutes, then serve.

To seduce someone

Ingredients:

- Three red rose petals.
- One teaspoon of yarrow yarrow.
- Two dried strawberries
- One teaspoon of dried violets;
- One vanilla bean;
- One teaspoon of honey.

Procedure:

1. Make 500 ml of water to heat.
2. Once hot, remove from heat and pour in all ingredients.
3. Let it rest 10 minutes, then serve.

To heal a broken heart

Ingredients:

- One teaspoon of black tea.
- One teaspoon of white willow bark
- One teaspoon of dried lavender
- Half teaspoon of licorice powder
- Two teaspoons of sugar

Procedure:

1. Make 500 ml of water to heat.
2. Once hot, remove from heat and pour in all ingredients.
3. Let it rest 10 minutes, then serve.

To gain wisdom

Ingredients:

- One teaspoon of black tea.
- One teaspoon of dried sage
- A teaspoon of peach flower.
- One slice of lemon
- One teaspoon of sugar

Procedure:

1. Make 500 ml of water to heat.
2. Once hot, remove from heat and pour in all ingredients.
3. Let it rest 10 minutes, then serve.

To bring mental clarity

Ingredients:
- One teaspoon of dried mint.
- A sprig of rosemary
- Dried peels of half a bergamot.
- One slice of lemon
- Two teaspoons of apple cider

Procedure:
1. Make 500 ml of water to heat.
2. Once hot, remove from heat and pour in all ingredients.
3. Let stand 10 minutes, then serve.

To strengthen your health

Ingredients:
- One teaspoon of orange flowers.
- Half teaspoon of nutmeg
- A sprig of thyme
- One teaspoon of dried mint
- Two teaspoons of honey

Procedure:
1. Make 500 ml of water to heat.
2. Once hot, remove from heat and pour in all ingredients.
3. Let it rest 10 minutes, then serve.

To break the evil eye

Ingredients:
- One teaspoon of elderberry filower.
- One teaspoon of lavender
- One teaspoon of yarrow yarrow
- One teaspoon of dried mugwort summits
- One teaspoon of sugar

Procedure:
1. Make 500 ml of water to heat.
2. Once hot, remove from heat and pour in all ingredients.
3. Let it rest 10 minutes, then serve.

To get good luck

Ingredients:
- Half teaspoon of cinnamon.
- One teaspoon of dried linden filters
- Half teaspoon of nutmeg
- Half teaspoon of pimenta dioica
- Two teaspoons of sugar

Procedure:
1. Put 500 ml of water to heat.
2. Once hot, remove from heat and pour in all ingredients.
3. Let it rest 10 minutes, then serve.

To break jealousy

Ingredients:

- Five dried chamomile fires.
- Five dandelion filters.
- Two sage leaves
- A sprig of lavender
- One orange flower

Procedure:

1. Make 500 ml of water to heat.
2. Once hot, remove from heat and pour in all ingredients.
3. Let it rest 10 minutes, then serve.

To tackle laziness

Ingredients:

- Five orange files.
- Five bergamot leaves
- 10 blueberries
- A sprig of peppermint

Procedure:

1. Make 500 ml of water to heat.
2. Once hot, remove from heat and pour in all ingredients.
3. Let it rest 10 minutes, then serve.

To break avarice

Ingredients:
- 10 dried lime tree flowers.
- 10 jasmine flowers
- 2 flowers of mallow
- 1 teaspoon of dandelion honey

Procedure:
1. Make 500 ml of water to heat.
2. Once hot, remove from heat and pour in all ingredients.
3. Let it rest 10 minutes, then serve.

To achieve inner calm

Ingredients:
- A sprig of dried lavender.
- 10 chamomile flowers.
- 3 leaves of dried sage
- One chasteberry flower

Procedure:
1. Make 500 ml of water to heat.
2. Once hot, remove from heat and pour in all ingredients.
3. Allow to stand 10 minutes, then serve.

To improve inner balance

Ingredients:

- 50 grams of fresh ginger.
- 10 grams of valerian root powder
- 10 grams of Asclepias tuberosa root.
- A sprig of thyme

Procedure:

1. Put 500 ml of water to heat.
2. Once hot, remove from heat and pour in all ingredients.
3. Let stand 10 minutes, then serve.

Final Thoughts

In this chapter, we looked at how to collect and store herbs to avoid waste, honor nature and know the plants and their parts.

The main herbs and magical plants used in Witchcraft practice were listed in the subchapter devoted to the witch's herbarium. You can use the herbarium as a guide to create your potions and recipes as soon as you feel ready to try your hand at creating them. Next, the best-known toxic herbs were explained, with a brief historical overview of each and its properties. The second part of the chapter presented ten magical infusion recipes with highly beneficial properties that are easy to prepare and within the reach of anyone. In the next chapter we will go deeper into the world of natural wellness remedies and what it means to be a natural healer.

Chapter 5
Become a Natural Healer

When you decide to embark on the fascinating path of Green Magic, there are countless physical and spiritual benefits you can derive from nature. It, as we have seen, is imbued with peace and tranquility. If you can connect with it, your physical body learns to untie itself from concepts such as time, anxiety and worries- all things that nature does not know, because it knows that it is perfect just as it is.

By connecting with nature, however, you are not the only person who can enjoy its immense benefits. By learning to master herbs and plants, you will be able to create recipes and potions that can help improve other people's lives. Those who practice this skill are defined as Natural Healers.

To understand the basis of the natural healer's work, it is good to first delve into what healing is. Healing is the reharmonization of an imbalance. Anxiety, worry, anger, sadness, jealousy are all emotional imbalances that can only be healed through a rebalancing of energies. The natural healer works to help you realign your energies to reharmonize with nature, and thus return to a state of peace and serenity.

The healing process takes place in two stages:

1. Cleansing of negative energies;

2. Infusion of new pure and positive energies.

These two phases are inseparable and indivisible. If one were to limit oneself to phase one, one would get an emotional void, not a positive vibrational state. If one were to limit oneself to phase two, on the other hand, no results would be achieved, since a glass filled with dirty water cannot contain even a drop of clean water. Therefore, it is necessary to cleanse the negative energies and then have an empty container inside which positive energies can be instilled. In this chapter we will see what types and methods of taking natural magic remedies are and present some natural remedies for your and your loved ones' well-being.

Consumption methods of natural magic remedies

Infusion

To make an infusion, simply bring water to a boil in a pot. Once the water starts to boil, turn off the heat and add the chosen herb mixture. Cover the pot with a lid and let it sit for at least ten minutes, then consume. The infusion can be drunk hot or allowed to cool and enjoy with ice. For infusions, it is best to prefer tender herbs and flowers that can easily release their properties.

Decoctions

Decoctions are best for herbs and hard plants, which require prolonged cooking to release their properties. The herb mixture should be placed in a pot filled with cold water (one liter of water for every 60g of plant part), then bring the water to a boil and let it cook for 10 to 15 minutes more. Once ready strain the mixture and store in glass containers.

Oils (non-food use)

Fresh or dried herbs, fires and leaves can be used to prepare an oil. Place the chosen set of herbs in an amber jar, then pour in extra virgin olive oil □nely to cover and seal the jar. Expose the jar to moonlight for fourteen days, making sure the place of exposure is dry and away from any source of moisture, or to sunlight as long as it is not direct. After two weeks have elapsed, strain the oil into another glass jar and store it waiting to be used. This procedure applies only to magic oils. The process for flavored oils intended for food use require an entirely different procedure.

Tinctures

Contrary to the name suggests, tinctures have nothing to do with dyeing. Mother tinctures are made by steeping one dried plant in ten parts ethyl alcohol in a glass container. Vodka is an ideal product because it contains few additives, while rum's strong flavor helps mask some herbs' unpleasant flavor. Once prepared, the mother tincture should be placed in a sealed jar and kept in a dark room, such as a cellar, for 21 days, shaking it once a day. After the steeping period is over, the tincture should be filtered, after which the resulting extract should be placed in amber glass containers and stored for a couple of years or more. Tinctures usually have a more pronounced effect than herbal teas and decoctions. Still, possessing a very high alcohol content, they cannot be drunk as a normal beverage: they must be taken with an eyedropper and diluted in water or beverages of preference, a maximum of 5ml at a time. It is advisable to take the tincture away from meals.

Pouches

Pouches are very effective talismans. You can keep them in your pocket, your purse, a drawer, behind a door, and anywhere we want its effectiveness. They are a small cloth pouch into which herbs are placed. They are quick and easy to make. To prepare a bag with herbs, you use a square of cloth colored in a color corresponding to your magical need, inside of which you will place herbs. It is recommended not to use more than three herbs simultaneously to avoid conflicts or cancellations between powers.

Take a square amount of cloth (the important thing is that it is 100 percent natural) of your chosen color and the loaded herb mix. To charge the herbs, simply make a prayer or recite a few phrases that charge the herbs with intentionality, and you can also use incense to strengthen your words.

After incanting, place the herbs in the center of the fabric, close the fabric on itself and tie it with a string or yarn of the same color. The smaller the bags, the easier they will be to carry. However, those intended to be hung around the house can be larger.

Baths

Baths are often used in Green Magic as they are an easy way to tap into the power of herbs by spreading it over one's body and infusing it into one's mind. To make a magical bath, one can prepare an infusion of herbs and add it to the water in the bath. You can also add essential oils to the water, but if you have delicate skin it is best to be careful about the amount.

Incenses

You can also enjoy the benefits of herbs through fumigation. To create simple incenses, choose fresh, aromatic herbs such as sage, rosemary, lavender, lemon leaves, etc., and make a bunch that will be tied and hung []xed until completely dried. Once dried, you will simply chop up the herbs and arrange them on a charcoal disc, which will be arranged on an incense burner (or a fireproof sand dish). You must know that although this is a natural incense, it is not a good idea to breathe its fumes or keep it burning in an enclosed room. Always air the room well when you have an incense burning, and keep it at least a couple of feet away from you.

Terapeutic Herbs

Unlike the herbarium contained in Chapter 3, where the plants and herbs most commonly used for magical purposes are listed, here the therapeutic properties of the herbs that natural healers rely on to create natural and herbal remedies will be explained. Natural healers devote their knowledge and efforts to learn deeply about the natural world and use its magnificent properties to benefit people. Spiritual healing, as well as physical healing, is a path, a journey. There is no magic concoction that can cure you of every ailment overnight. Although medicinal herbs have a great deal of efficacy at the level of physical healing, it cannot do the same for spiritual healing except through the full awareness of the person who wants to heal. The natural healer is concerned with the psychophysical well-being of those who require his or her skills, going far beyond offering a miraculous infusion, working in the unconscious and the spirit of the person so that evil can be driven out space made for good. In this chapter you will find some natural wellness remedies natural healers use to heal body and mind. Feel free to try to replicate these recipes, perhaps trying them on yourself first first until you feel something change within you. But remember: no remedy is truly efficient if there is no will and intentionality.

- Yarrow: anticoagulant
- Laurel: diuretic, digestive, expectorant.
- Garlic: antiseptic, antibiotic.
- Holly: diuretic, depurative.
- Artemisia: sedative, antiseptic.
- Basil: diuretic, anti-inflammatory, sedative.
- Birch: depurative, draining.
- Camellia: antioxidant, antifungal.
- Chamomile: antimicrobial, antiseptic, antibacterial, anti-inflammatory, carminative, spasmolytic, healing.

- Cinnamon: antiseptic, eupeptic, gastrointestinal spasms.
- Cardamom: antidote against snake and scorpion venom, eupeptic.
- Clove: invigorating, antioxidant.
- Cherry: laxative, diuretic, draining.
- Coriander: carminative.
- Cumin: antioxidant, hepatoprotective.
- Dittamo: diuretic, digestive, antispasmodic, astringent, calming.
- Ivy: anti-inflammatory, anti-cellulite.
- Heather: diuretic, antirheumatic, anti-inflammatory.
- Fig: laxative, invigorating.
- Wild fennel: depurative, anticolic, antispasmodic.
- Strawberry: antioxidant, antitumor, laxative.
- Jasmine: anti-stress, antioxidant.
- Juniper: diuretic, anti-inflammatory, antiviral.
- Hypericum: antidepressant, calming.
- Hyssop: balsamic, bronchodilator.
- Lavender: analgesic, antibacterial, sedative, hypotensive.
- Licorice: digestive, anti-inflammatory, hypertensive.
- Pomegranate: gastroprotective, vasoprotective, antioxidant.
- Mint: anesthetic, analgesic, decongestant.
- Myrtle: balsamic, astringent.
- Moss: disinfectant, healing.
- Walnut: antioxidant, anti-inflammatory, digestive.
- Nutmeg: digestive, carminative.
- Nettle: antirheumatic, antianemic, diuretic, vasoconstrictor.
- Chili pepper: vasodilator, cardioprotective, disinfectant.
- Blackthorn: diuretic, depurative, antioxidant.
- Rose: soothing, anti-wrinkle, anti-inflammatory.
- Rosemary: antiemetic, antirheumatic. Elderberry: diuretic, immune defense.

- Sage: antiseptic, carminative, astringent, antisudorific.
- Sesame: remineralizing.
- Rowan: diuretic, soothing.
- Thyme: antimicrobial, antispasmodic.
- Verbena: disinfectant, healing, digestive.
- Saffron: eupeptic, antispasmodic, sedative.
- Ginger: digestive, antinausea, antinflammatory.

Essential Oils

Essential oils were known and widely used as early as ancient times, with written records dating back to 4500 BC. The Egyptians used essential oils in various fields, such as medicine, cosmetics, and even embalming rituals. Later the use of essential oils expanded to the Middle East around 4000 BC, and then to China around 2800 BC. Today essential oils are used in Witchcraft for various purposes: candle dressing, magical bathing, massage, oral intake, pouches and witch bottles. Essential oils can be obtained through two main so-called "natural" methods:

- Distillation;
- Maceration.

There are other methods of obtaining essential oils from plants. Still, these are mostly chemical or complicated processes that only specialized factories and companies can adopt to create oils in large quantities. This section will focus only on the best-known methods that can be easily replicated at home.

A Green witch must ensure that the ingredients used for rituals and spells are natural and free of artificial treatments. It is easy to get ripped off online and in stores, noticing bargain prices, but often the low price indicates the product's low purity. Some unserious companies add chemical or synthetic components to the compounds to increase the essential oil's aroma or lower its production cost. Essential oils can be very expensive, so it is good to be suspicious of those who sell them for a few euros, even though the label states "100% essential oil." Real essential oils are concentrated and only a few drops are needed to give off an intense, lingering scent, unlike perfumes. It is necessary always to be careful what you buy and, if possible, to create as much at home and by yourself to avoid falling for scams that, in addition to hurting your wallet, would lead to ineffective or even counterproductive spells and remedies. Let's see together what the two main methods are for extracting essential oils from plants, although the one that offers the purest and most satisfactory result is only one: distillation.

Distillation

Essential oils through distillation are obtained using a steam current distiller. The process is as follows:

1. Plants to be distilled (fresh or dried) are collected in a hermetically sealed container.

2. Water vapor fluices into the container and breaks up the plant tissues of the plants, which release the essential oil that mixes with the vapor.

3. The steam and oil are passed through a coil to cool the mixture.

4. Through the coil, the steam becomes water. The essential oils, which have a different specific weight than water, separate and are made to fluire in a different container.

5. We have thus extracted the essential oil.

However, not everyone owns a distiller or plans to buy one, given the cost and bulk. Therefore, the maceration technique, which we now see, is used more in DIY.

Maceration

Something similar to essential oil can also be obtained through maceration: the correct name for the product is "oleolite," although many still define it as essential oil. Oleolite is a lighter and less pure version of essential oil, and it uses infusion in vegetable oil to extract the essential oil of plants.

The process is very short and easy to perform:

1. Choose the mixture of herbs to be macerated and pound them in a mortar to release their essential oils.

2. Place the crushed herbs in a glass container with a stopper and fill with vegetable oil.

3. Allow to macerate for 48 hours, then strain with cotton gauze. If the oil is not sufficiently flavored, the process can be repeated by adding new herbs and letting the oil macerate for another 48 hours as often as you deem necessary.

You can start making your essential oils and oleolites right away by consulting the Witch's Herbarium in Chapter 3, so you can learn about the magical properties of the plants and choose the ones that are suitable for your purpose.

Herbal Healing Decoctions

Inluuence with fever

Ingredients:

- 30 grams of eucalyptus leaves
- 30 grams of thyme leaves
- 30 grams of bark of white willow
- 30 grams of lime filters
- 10 grams of calamus root
- 500ml water

Procedure:

1. Mix the herbs separately, pounding them in a mortar if necessary.
2. Place a pot with half a liter of water on the stove. When it boils, add the ingredients
3. previously prepared.
4. Allow to steep in boiling water for 10 minutes, then turn off the heat.
5. Strain through a colander and consume while still hot before bedtime.

Cold

Ingredients:

- Juice of one lemon
- Peels of an untreated lemon
- One clove of garlic
- One tablespoon of eucalyptus honey (or balsamic honey)
- 500ml water

Procedure:

1. Cut the garlic into rounds and put it in a container along with the juice of a freshly squeezed lemon and its peels.

2. Place a pot with half a liter of water on the stove. When it boils, add the ingredients previously prepared.

3. Allow to steep in boiling water for 10 minutes, then turn off the heat.

4. Strain the drink through a strainer, then serve it in a cup by adding a spoon of honey of eucalyptus or balsamic.

5. Consume piping hot, inhaling the fumes.

Nausea

Ingredients:

- Juice of half a lemon
- 20 grams of fresh ginger
- One bay leaf
- A sprig of peppermint
- 500ml water

Procedure:

1. Cut ginger into rounds and put it in a cup with half a freshly squeezed lemon, bay leaf and peppermint juice.

2. Place a pot with half a liter of water on the stove. When it boils, add the ingredients previously prepared.

3. Allow to steep in boiling water for 15 minutes, then turn off the heat.
4. Strain the drink through a strainer, then serve in a cup, sweetening to taste.
5. It is possible to consume it either hot or cold.

Digestion issues

Ingredients:

- Juice of half a lemon
- 20 grams of fresh ginger
- Half teaspoon of pistils of saffron
- 20 grams of sage
- 500ml water

Procedure:

1. Cut the ginger into rounds and put it in a cup along with the juice of half a freshly squeezed lemon, sage and saffron.
2. Place a pot with half a liter of water on the stove. When it boils, add the ingredients previously prepared.
3. Allow to steep in boiling water for 15 minutes, then turn off the heat.
4. Strain the drink through a strainer, then serve in a cup and consume after meals.

Cough and Influence

Ingredients:

- Juice of half a lemon
- 1 red apple
- 1 bay leaf
- 2 dry fiks
- 3 lemon leaves
- 1 tablespoon of eucalyptus honey
- 500ml water

Procedure:

1. Cut the apple into pieces and remove the seeds.

2. Place a pot with half a liter of water on the stove. When it boils, add all the previously prepared ingredients.

3. Allow to steep in boiling water for 30 minutes, then turn off the heat.

4. Strain the drink through a strainer, serve it in a cup and consume hot as needed.

Antioxidant and vitaminizing decoction

Ingredients:

- Juice of one lemon
- 500 grams of dried hibiscus filters
- 50 grams of peppermint
- 5 orange filters
- 500ml water

Procedure:

1. Pound orange blossoms with peppermint in a mortar, add hibiscus blossomos and lemon juice, and mix.

2. Place a pot with half a liter of water on the stove. When it boils, add all the previously prepared ingredients.

3. Allow to steep in boiling water for 15 minutes, then turn off the heat.

4. Strain the drink through a strainer, serve it in a cup and consume hot or cold as needed.

Purifying decoction

Ingredients:

- 50 grams of dandelion root
- 50 grams of burdock root
- 20 grams official fumaria

- 20 grams of peppermint
- 500ml water

Procedure:

1. Place a pot with half a liter of water on the stove. When it boils, add all the previously prepared ingredients.

2. Allow to steep in boiling water for 15 minutes, then turn off the heat.

3. Strain the drink through a strainer, then serve it in a cup and consume hot, preferably away from meals.

Draining decoction

Ingredients:

- 50 grams of leaves of dried artichoke
- 20 grams of peppermint
- 15 grams of lemon balm leaves
- 500ml water

Procedure:

1. Place a pot with half a liter of water on the stove. When it boils, add all the previously prepared ingredients.

2. Allow to steep in boiling water for 15 minutes, then turn off the heat.

3. Strain the drink through a strainer, then serve it in a cup and consume hot, preferably away from meals.

Soothing decoction for inflammations

Ingredients:

- 20 grams of mallow fish and leaves
- 20 untreated rose petals
- 20 dandelion filters
- 1 liter of water

Procedure:

1. Place a pot with one liter of water on the stove. When it boils, add all the previously prepared ingredients.

2. Allow to steep in boiling water for 15 minutes, then turn off the heat.

3. Strain the drink through a strainer, then store it in a suitable container. This decoction is excellent for soothing skin reddened by sunburn, eczema, and is also an excellent remedy for cystitis when used to make intimate douches. It can also be drunk: in this case it will help diuresis and intestinal well-being.

Energizing and stimulating decoction

Ingredients:

- 1 red apple
- 100 grams of strawberries
- 5 cloves
- 1 cinnamon stick
- 5 grams of dried green tea
- 1 liter of water

Procedure:

1. Cut the apple in chunks and remove the seeds.

2. Cut the strawberries in half.

3. Place a pot with one liter of water on the stove. When it boils, add all the previously prepared ingredients.

4. Allow to steep in boiling water for 20 minutes, then turn off the heat.

5. Strain the drink through a strainer, then serve in a cup, sweetening to taste.

Magickal Pouches

To ward off negative energies

Ingredients:
- A small brown cloth bag
- A red ribbon
- A moonstone
- 9 grams of dried lavender
- 9 grams of dried bay leaves
- 3 cinnamon sticks

Procedure:
1. Place all the herbs in the small bag along with the moonstone.

2. Close the small bag and fix it with ribbon. The number of knots should be odd (3 is the ideal number).

3. Carry the pouch with you fixed for up to 14 days, then replace the herbs and recharge the stone.

To strengthen your love bond

Ingredients:
- A small red cloth bag
- A red ribbon
- Three dried rose rose petals
- A sprig of dried lavender
- A rose quartz
- A shell

Procedure:
1. Place all the herbs in the small bag along with the rose quartz and shell.

2. Close the small bag and fix it with ribbon. The number of knots should be odd (3 is the ideal number).

3. Carry the pouch with you fixed for up to 14 days, then replace the herbs and recharge the stone.

To raise financial well-being

Ingredients:
- A small white silk bag
- A red ribbon
- Seven narcissus petals
- Seven one-cent coins
- Seven grains of wheat

Procedure:
1. Place all the herbs in the small bag along with the coins.
2. Close the small bag and fix it with ribbon. The number of knots should be odd (3 is the ideal number).
3. Take the pouch with you fixed for up to 14 days, then replace the herbs.

To foster spiritual enlightenment

Ingredients:
- A small white silk bag
- A red ribbon
- Seven dried white rose petals
- A hyaline quartz
- 5 grams of dried henbane (warning: poisonous plant)

Procedure:
1. Place all the herbs in the small bag along with the hyaline quartz.
2. Close the small bag and fix it with ribbon. The number of knots should be odd (3 is the ideal number).
3. Carry the pouch with you fixed for up to 14 days, then replace the herbs and recharge the stone.

To propitiate prosperity

Ingredients:
- A small green cloth bag
- A golden ribbon
- A cinnamon stick
- 6 honeysuckle filters
- 6 cloves
- A jade stone

Procedure:
1. Place all the herbs in the small bag along with the jade.
2. Close the small bag and fix it with ribbon making six tight knots.
3. Carry the pouch with you fixed for up to 14 days, then replace the herbs and recharge the stone.

To healing spiritual wounds

Ingredients:
- A small blue cloth bag
- A red ribbon
- A linden leaf
- A sprig of chasteberry
- A handful of moss
- A rock crystal

Procedure:
1. Place all the herbs in the small bag along with the rock crystal.
2. Close the small bag and fix it with ribbon. The number of knots should be odd (3 is the ideal number).
3. Carry the pouch with you fixed for up to 14 days, then replace the herbs and recharge the stone.

To deepen gratitude

Ingredients:
- A small yellow cloth bag
- A white ribbon
- Three ivy leaves
- A sprig of peppermint
- 9 sunflower seeds
- A black tourmaline stone

Procedure:
1. Place all the herbs in the small bag along with the black tourmaline.

2. Close the small bag and fix it with ribbon. The number of knots should be odd (3 is the ideal number).

3. Carry the pouch with you fixed for up to 14 days, then replace the herbs and recharge the stone.

To instill self-confidence

Ingredients:
- An orange silk bag
- A pink ribbon
- A sprig of rosemary
- A sprig of dried lavender
- 3 orange filters
- An agate stone

Procedure:
1. Place all the herbs in the small bag along with the agate.

2. Close the small bag and fix it with ribbon. The number of knots should be odd (3 is the ideal number).

3. Carry the pouch with you fixed for up to 14 days, then replace the herbs and recharge the stone.

To develop a magnetic appeal

Ingredients:
- A small red silk bag
- A red ribbon
- 5 dried basil leaves
- 5 chunks of one dried chili pepper
- 5 pinches of paprika
- 5 pinches of nutmeg
- 5 cloves

Procedure:
1. Place all the herbs and spices in the small bag.
2. Close the small bag and fix it with ribbon. The number of knots should be odd (5 is the ideal number in this case).
3. Carry the pouch with you fixed up to 14 days at heart height, then substitute herbs as needed.

To develop self-control

Ingredients:
- A small white silk bag
- A red ribbon
- 3 red chilies
- 3 pinches of coarse salt
- 3 bergamot leaves
- 1 green aventurine stone

Procedure:
1. Place all the herbs and spices in the small bag and green aventurine.
2. Close the small bag and fix it with ribbon. The number of knots should be odd (5 is the ideal number in this case).
3. Carry the pouch with you fixed up to 14 days at heart height, then substitute herbs as needed.

Magickal Elixirs

To induce sound sleep

Ingredients:

- 100 grams of dried chamomile flowers
- 1 liter of water
- 500 grams of sugar
- 200 grams 95° alcohol
- 5 grams dried orange peel
- 5 grams of cinnamon

Procedure:

1. Place dried chamomile flowers, cinnamon and dried orange peel in an airtight container and let them macerate for one week in 200 grams of 95° alcohol, shaking occasionally.

2. Afterward, squeeze out the macerated herbs and pass the liquid through a filter.

3. Place one liter of water in a pot and 500 grams of sugar to medium heat, stirring continuously until a syrup's consistency is achieved.

4. Pour the syrup and the liquid obtained from steeping into a small bottle or glass container (preferably amber) and let it sit for a few days in a dark place.

5. Pour two teaspoons into a cup of lukewarm water and drink before bedtime.

To foster passionate love

Ingredients:

- 1 liter of cognac
- 50 grams of basil
- 50 grams of tarragon
- 50 grams of sage
- 50 grams rosemary
- 50 grams of thyme
- Peel of an untreated lemon

Procedure:

1. Place all the herbs in an airtight container along with the cognac and let macerate for at least 25 days.

2. On the 25th day of steeping, add the lemon peel and let it macerate for another 25 days.

3. Strain the mixture and store in an amber glass bottle for an additional 25 days.

4. After this time has elapsed, consume a shot glass as needed.

To calm body and mind

Ingredients:

- One liter of water
- 250 grams of 95° alcohol
- 500 grams of sugar
- 3 sprigs of lavender
- One teaspoon of dried St. John's Wort
- 5 untreated rose petals

Procedure:

1. Pound lavender and St. John's Wort leaves in a mortar.

2. Place the crushed herbs and rose petals in an airtight container and let ma-

cerate for a week in 250 grams of 95° alcohol, shaking occasionally.

3. Afterward, squeeze out the macerated herbs and pass the liquid through a filter.

4. Place one liter of water and 500 grams of sugar in a saucepan over medium fire, stirring continuously until a syrup's consistency is achieved.

5. Pour the syrup and the liquid obtained from steeping into a small bottle or glass container (preferably amber) and let it sit for a few days in a dark place.

6. Pour two teaspoons into a cup of lukewarm water and drink as needed. Taking more than two servings per day is not recommended.

To attract honesty and sincerity

Ingredients:

- One liter of water
- 250 grams of 95° alcohol
- 500 grams of sugar
- 30 grams of fresh peppermint
- 50 grams of dried lemongrass
- 100 grams of ginger

Procedure:

1. Pound peppermint and lemongrass in a mortar.

2. Place the crushed herbs and sliced ginger in an airtight container and let macerate for a week in 250 grams of 95° alcohol, shaking occasionally.

3. Afterward, squeeze out the macerated herbs and pass the liquid through a filter.

4. Place one liter of water and 500 grams of sugar in a saucepan over medium fire, stirring continuously until a syrup's consistency is achieved.

5. Pour the syrup and the liquid obtained from steeping into a small bottle or glass container (preferably amber) and let it sit for a few days in a dark place.

6. Because of the very strong and refreshing flavor, diluting the elixir in still or sparkling water is recommended at about 50 ml to one liter of water. Still, you can vary the dose as desired, always keeping in mind the high alcohol content.

To reverse mental and psychic fatigue

Ingredients:

- One liter of water
- 250 grams of 95° alcohol
- 500 grams of sugar
- 15 grams of juniper berries
- 30 grams of fresh peppermint
- 10 grams of eucalyptus
- Peel of an untreated grapefruit
- 50 grams of blueberries

Procedure:

1. Pound peppermint, eucalyptus and blueberries in a mortar.

2. Place the crushed herbs together with the juniper berries and grapefruit peels in an airtight container and let macerate for a week in 250 grams of 95° alcohol, shaking occasionally.

3. Afterward, squeeze out the macerated herbs and pass the liquid through a filter.

4. Place one liter of water and 500 grams of sugar in a saucepan over medium fire, stirring continuously until a syrup's consistency is achieved.

5. Pour the syrup and the liquid obtained from steeping into a small bottle or glass container (preferably amber) and let it sit for a few days in a dark place.

6. Pour two teaspoons into a cup of lukewarm water and drink as needed. Taking more than two servings per day is not recommended.

Final Thoughts

In this concluding chapter we learned what methods of taking natural remedies embrace all five senses of perception and are extremely adaptable to the preferences of the witch using them. We then delved into natural wellness remedies you can apply to yourself and others to aid physical and spiritual healing. You learned who a natural healer is and how their knowledge of the natural world can greatly benefit anyone's life. You have also learned the basics of becoming a natural healer yourself. Although this manual cannot, for obvious reasons, provide you with exhaustive training that qualifies you, it has introduced you to him and the steps you can take, right away, to embark on the path of natural healing. The road to becoming a natural healer is still long, but you have just taken a big step and, as the saying goes, those who begin well are half the work.

Conclusion

We have reached the finish of this manual, but your path to Witchcraft is only just beginning. With constant practice you will improve daily, and in no time you will become a green witch capable of creating your grimoire containing your recipes and natural wellness remedies. As you learned while reading this book, Green Magic is an age-old tradition that, if mastered correctly, can help you achieve incredible results. But don't be discouraged if results are slow to come first, because you will learn what works for you through practice. We are not all the same: what works for someone may be a failure for someone else. Every witch must have the chance to make mistakes; only then can she learn and improve herself.

Witchcraft is not just a practice, but a way of life, the conscious choice to pursue the path of magic to improve your own life and the lives of others. It is a path that begins from within yourself, from knowing yourself and your abilities. Only from deep familiarity with your power can the roots of a competence develop that will lead you to do great things. The magic begins with you. If you found this book useful and comprehensive, I ask you to take a minute to write an honest review on Amazon-it will be of immense help in spreading this book to more and more people and helping them to get closer to Witchcraft. If you have any useful tips, doubts or questions, please do not hesitate to voice them. Your opinion is important!

Printed in Great Britain
by Amazon